THIS
SCOUTING
LIFE

THIS SCOUTING LIFE

A Memoir of a Simpler Time

Archie Raeside

The History Press Ireland

First published 2012

The History Press Ireland
119 Lower Baggot Street
Dublin 2
Ireland
www.thehistorypress.ie

British Library Cataloguing in Publication Data.
A catalogue record for this book is available from the British Library.

ISBN 978 1 84588 733 9

Typesetting and origination by The History Press
Manufacturing managed by Jellyfish Print Solutions Ltd

CONTENTS

WHY SCOUTING?

Standing just head and shoulders above the living room windowsill, I watched and waited excitedly for Bill and Brendan Lawlor to come into view. While they were still a good distance away I knew it was them, because Bill, the older of the brothers, was wearing a distinctive Scout hat which looked just like a Canadian Mountie's. 'They're coming,' I called out and Mammy came through the kitchen door urging me to contain my excitement. It was more polite to wait until they came up the garden path and knocked on the hall door, Mammy said. 'We've come to take Archie to the Scouts,' said Bill. Mammy thanked them, and we set off to what was to be my first Cub Scout meeting, and the start of over half a century's involvement. This was 1947.

I'm not sure why I wanted to join the Scouts. Football and hurling at school and being an altar server at the local church somehow did not seem enough though, and Drimnagh, where I lived at that time, had few organised facilities for young people. I think I was looking for something more interesting, or perhaps it was the fact that my father had been a Scout in Scotland for a number of years. His first visit to Ireland was with his group of Rover Scouts. Perhaps I was influenced by pictures in the family photo album of him and his mates camping at Powerscourt Demesne. At seven years old the idea of travelling to remote areas to experience living in a forest or on a mountainside appealed to me and this was what the Scouts seemed to offer.

My parents had obviously made enquiries as to the whereabouts of local Scout Troops and the closest to our house was at Merchants Quay, about three miles away. There were so few troops established that my name went on the waiting list. Mother had befriended a Mrs Lawlor who lived close to our church and discovered that her boys were in the Scouts attached to the parish of Donore Avenue. So it was that I now found myself on my way with Bill and Brendan to the Scout hall.

Although the troop, known as St Theresa's Troop 35th Dublin, was founded in Donore Avenue nineteen years earlier, the meeting place would change many times in its long history. Fr Valentine Burke, head curate of St Theresa's church, Donore Avenue founded it in 1928. The first Scoutmaster (now termed Scout Leader) was Mr Jack Giltrap. He was a former Baden-Powell Rover Scout. He had long left the unit when I joined but many years later I would meet up with him, as we both worked for the same company (Fry Cadbury) for a few years. At that time it was usual for Protestant boys who had a spirit of adventure to join the SAI (Scout Association of Ireland) or the Boys Brigade (BB), of which my uncle Ian and cousins Bobby and Duggy were members. Catholic boys with like-minds joined the CBSI (Catholic Boy Scouts of Ireland). We referred to the SAI as Baden-Powell Scouts. Of course we were all following in the great tradition of the world brotherhood of Scouting as envisaged and established by Lord Baden-Powell.

It is generally accepted that, sometime in 1928, Fr Burke acquired the use of the Little Flower Hall in Meath Street for troop meetings and, under his aegis, the troop was well provided for. He was known locally as 'Toucher Burke' because of his ability to extract money for any useful purpose. There is a story about a child who swallowed a halfpenny and after the doctor was unsuccessful in removing it, neighbours advised his parents to take the child to Fr Burke because he could get money out of anyone. In 1947, Fr Burke was appointed to the National Executive of CBSI.

About this time, however, he was transferred as parish priest to Cabra West and lost to our unit. Following his departure, notice was given to vacate the Little Flower Hall. With this began a period of moving about from one meeting place to another, and it was also, more significantly for me, the point at which I became an official member.

With the Lawlor brothers as my escort, we crossed the bridge near my house, then a short distance along the canal tow path and over the footbridge at the 2nd Lock. Now in

Inchicore parish we hurried along Connolly Avenue on to Emmet Road, then turned right on to Grattan Crescent at the north end of Tyrconnell Road. The final leg of the journey was along Inchicore Terrace which led to the Inchicore Railway works. The troop had acquired the use of the railway dining hall for their meetings. The troop had two sections then: the Cubs (known as the Cub Pack) and the Scouts.

Once inside the Den, Brendan, who was Senior Sixer', introduced me to the Cub Master, Mr Healy. Leaders' surnames were prefixed with 'Mister' or they were addressed as 'Sir' back then, and it would have been considered cheeky and even disrespectful to use first names when addressing adults.

To become a member of the 'Pack' it was necessary to be eight years of age or to have made your First Holy Communion, and to pass a few tests. I soon learned the promise, the principles and the Cub prayer. So as to be ready for the 'investiture' ceremony it was also necessary to learn 'foot-drill'. The weekly meetings began with the Cub prayer followed by collection of subs, which were only a few pence, and then an activity game.

The games varied from week to week and were designed to heighten our senses and develop physical strength. 'Snatch the Bacon' or 'Pirate Chief' was always a firm favourite. After lining up to form three sides of a square, one blindfolded boy sat in the centre of the fourth side with legs crossed. From the beginning of one line, each in turn called out his position until everyone had a number. One of the leaders then placed a Cub cap just in front of the seated player; this represented the bacon. When a number was called out, the challenge was for the selected player to reach and 'snatch the bacon' and return to the line before being pointed at by the blindfolded player known as the pirate. To do this there had to be absolute silence so as to be fair to the pirate chief in detecting the approach of the thief and also to test the dexterity of the later. If pointed at, then the thief took up the position of the pirate.

'The Box' was a bit more physical. A large circle was formed by holding hands and a box was placed in the centre of the circle. The leader then called out 'To the right!' or 'To the left!' and the entire circle of players, still holding hands, ran as fast as they could. At will, the strongest players pulled those nearest them towards the box and if made to hit the box that player was out. Should two players loose their grip during the run, then they were both out.

The game 'Bulldog' also required everyone to be 'numbered off' and this time the participants lined up across the room. One player, the bulldog, was chosen to stand facing the group some distance away. The bulldog called out a number and that player had to reach the opposite end of the room without being caught. If the bulldog failed to catch the player, then the entire group raced to the other end of the room. The bulldog then had a second opportunity to catch a player or two. When caught, a player joined forces with the bulldog. Eventually there would be only one or two left against the rest and there was seldom an outright winner.

After these physical games, we were happy to take instruction in first aid, compass points, knots or nature study. Some meetings finished with campfire songs. Everybody knew the Troop Yell and the Troop Song, as these were always a part of the campfire. The tradition of campfire singing had begun almost at the founding of the troop and was to become well known within the organisation.

2

35TH DUBLIN, EARLY YEARS

In the years preceding my involvement with the 35th Dublin, they had been active in many notable areas, not least of these being the Eucharistic Congress in June 1932 where they were involved in stewarding and providing first-aid facilities.

A huge Scout pilgrimage to Rome was organised by the CBSI in 1934 and the 35th Dublin was well represented there with fifteen members taking part. The pilgrims, led by his Eminence Cardinal McRory, Archbishop of Armagh and Primate of All-Ireland, travelled aboard the luxury liner *Lancastria*. Accompanying the group was William T. Cosgrave, TD and Sir Martin Melvin. William Cosgrave had been President of the Executive Council of the Irish Free State for ten years (later to become Taoiseach) and was a personal friend of the Chief Scout, Prof. Whelehan. Sir Martin Melvin had decided to present a costly trophy to CBSI for inter-troop competition and had commissioned the leading silversmith of the time, Miss Mia Cranwell, to produce it. In a ceremony aboard the *Lancastria*, he formally presented the handsome silver trophy to the Chief Scout.

Each troop had a flag, ours was borne by a great Scouter, Nicky Donegan, and the array of flags obviously impressed Pope Pius XI because at the end of the ceremonies in the Throne Room, he inspected them all. When he came to flag of the 35th, he asked for it to be unfurled. Anyone who has seen this flag will know just what a work of art it was. A silk embroidered figure of St Theresa and the Little Flower by the Sisters of Charity in Donore Avenue, in the finest gold, silver and many coloured threads was featured on one side, the Scout Badge and scroll on the other. The colours were blessed on Whit Sunday 1933 by the parish priest, Canon Hayes. The following was recorded in the *Catholic Scout* in 1933, 'The flag is a credit to Irish workmanship, being made by Messrs. Bull and Co. It was a gift of a few friends who prefer to remain anonymous.' Scout Troops from Rathmines, Clonsilla, SS Micheal and John's, Merchants Quay, Dolphin's Barn, Halston Street and Whitefriar Street, accompanied by their bands, attended the ceremony. For forty-two years the flag was flown with pride but the long years of service caused it to need replacement. I will come to the fate of the original flag later.

Nicky Donegan became Scoutmaster later that year and stayed in that post until 1939, when, after the Second World War had started, Nicky went to Belfast on the 12 October and joined the Irish Guards, leaving for London that same night.

At Larch Hill National Campsite of Scouting Ireland, on 21 August 2004, I met veterans of the 1934 trip to Rome and many of my former Scouting colleagues. The event was organised principally for the three following reasons:

- To bring together the two great Scouting traditions (CBSI and SAI) in the new association Scouting Ireland.

- To celebrate the British–Irish links and friendship, which have always endured in Scouting, even in the darkest days.

- To remember the tragedy of the HMT *Lancastria* and to celebrate its contribution in Scouting in Ireland and its role in securing Larch Hill for Scouting.

The connection between the *Lancastria* and Larch Hill is that Larch Hill was purchased largely through the profits which the Association made on the fares of the non-Scout pilgrims to Rome. At that time, 1937-8, CBSI was preoccupied with the need for a national campsite. The search eventually narrowed down to two possible locations: part of Santry Park, north of Dublin City and an estate near Tibradden called Larch Hill on the foothills of the Dublin Mountains, not far from the border with County Wicklow.

When you compare the natural and unspoiled nature of the Larch Hill site with all it has to offer young people, they certainly made the correct decision over seventy years ago.

A short history of the ship is in the Commemoration booklet prepared for the ceremony at Larch Hill and goes as follows:

The 16,243-tonne Cunard liner was built by William Beardmore & Co., Dalmuir, Glasgow, making her maiden voyage under the name of *Tyrrhenia*, from Glasgow to Montreal on 13 June 1922.

Refitted just two years later with a plush new interior and a new name, *Lancastria*, she spent many years leisurely sailing the world's oceans. Her final peacetime cruise in the idyllic waters of the Bahamas was made in September 1939 and ended with the ship docked in New York and the world at war.

Here she underwent a radical change – her portholes were blacked out, drab grey military paint daubed all over her and guns mounted near to the once splendid swimming pool. Her cruising days were over forever as she took on the role of one of Her Majesty's troopships.

At 0400 hrs on 17 June 1940 she anchored slightly off Saint Nazaire at Charpentier Roads and began evacuating soldiers from the British Expeditionary Force along with some RAF men and a few civilians.

There is no completely accurate figure for the number aboard but it is estimated at a little over 7,000 people. Four bombs hit in total. One was a bull's eye, dropping straight down the funnel and exploding in the engine room. At 4.15 p.m., less than twenty minutes later, the *Lancastria* rolled onto her port side and made her way, bow first, to her grave on the seabed.

The crew and passengers appeared not to panic while abandoning the sinking liner and, incredibly, singing was heard as the ship went down ('Roll Out the Barrel' and 'There Will Always Be An England'). It is estimated between 4,500 and 5,000 people died that day. Thankfully, however, this left around 2,500 people who were rescued. One reason that *Lancastria* history is not well known is that Winston Churchill felt the country's morale could not bear the burden of such terrible news, and newspapers were ordered not to print the story. The *Lancastria* lies in 26 meters of water off St Nazaire.

To return to my first meeting, Mr Healy welcomed me and explained what it was to be a Cub Scout. In my experience he was liked by every Cub in the pack and had what I can only describe as a special gift of being able to make each individual Cub feel special. His assistant, Dermot Richardson, was of a similar manner and he tutored me in the requirements for qualification. It wasn't too long before all the tests were passed. Eventually the big day arrived and I was ready. Two lines of Scouts formed up facing each other on two sides of the hall and us Cub Scouts formed a line across the end, completing a U-shape of the full troop. At the open end of this formation, the leaders took up their positions. Immediately in front of the leaders a flag bearer held the Troop Flag in a horizontal position. The Scouts, some of them new members of the troop and some former Cubs, were first to be 'invested'. We were, of course, practised in the ceremonial procedure at a couple of weekly meetings previously. Just like everyone else, when my turn came I marched smartly up to the flag and placed my left hand on it. At the same time I raised my right hand to shoulder height, making the Cub Scout sign with my right hand, and recited the 'Cub Scout Promise'. Coming to attention, the official blue and yellow neckerchief was placed around my neck and the uniform cap on my head by Mr Healy. We exchanged salutes and I about-turned and returned to my 'Six' as a fully-fledged Cub Scout.

Our Cub Pack had about forty members between the ages of eight and eleven years. The membership was subdivided into groups of six. Each 'Six' was allocated a colour by which they were identified and each Cub wore a triangular badge of the appropriate colour on the upper left sleeve of his uniform sweater. In charge of each 'Six' was a 'Sixer' (appropriately enough) and he had the distinction of wearing two yellow stripes on his sleeve. He had an assistant to help him who proudly wore one yellow stripe. The overall boy leader or Senior Sixer was distinguished by three stripes and he was seen to be the link between the members of the pack and the adult leaders. This gave him a unique standing within the pack and was regarded by us new recruits as a 'Super Cub'. When I joined, this elite Cub was Brendan Lawlor and his cousin Robert was my 'Sixer'.

Outdoor activities played an important part of the programme throughout the year and so an appreciation of the changing faces of nature in all seasons was acquired. We went hiking on one or two Sundays a month to Larch Hill or the Pine Forrest on the outskirts of Dublin where we learned to prepare and light cooking fires. An important part of this skill was to leave the site with no trace of having been there. Sometimes cooking skills were learned the hard way. On one occasion, a Cub placed his unopened can of beans in a Billy Can of water on the fire, not aware of the consequences. When the can exploded, raining beans upon us, he was quick to learn that this was not the correct method.

Winter hiking was particularly popular, perhaps because it tended to be more challenging. For a start, it was more difficult to find dry kindling to get a cooking fire going and keep it going if the weather changed to rain. Dinner plates were great for fanning a fire and keep up a good blaze. Snow was a different matter because, after the meal, we would have snowball fights or slide down the frozen snow-covered slopes on our enamelled steel dinner plates. The enamel on the plate soon became chipped from this unconventional use and the exposed metal rusted, which did not please our parents. Plates and mugs later became available which were made from aluminium and then plastic, which greatly reduced the rate of destruction.

For an eight-year-old boy, a night or two away from family and home was exciting. To spend it in the mountains was an adventure. I'm sure most people will never forget their first camping weekend. None of the fancy designer hiking and camping equipment that is now available existed. Some ex-military tents and haversacks were available but, as the Second World War was not long ended, some of this was in short supply in Ireland. Father had obtained a sailor's knapsack, which was to be my haversack. With checklist in hand, Mother called out the items one by one and I scanned the array of items on the floor. 'Blankets and blanket pins?' I replied 'Ok'. 'Spare socks?' 'Ok.' 'Towel and soap?' 'Ok.' And so it went on until she reached the end of the list which included all clothing and food items necessary to survive the weekend. With everything packed I lifted the bulging knapsack on to my left shoulder and staggered under the weight. 'You should drive him to Aston's Quay, he'll never manage that lot,' said Mother. Father replied, 'Ach, he'll be grand, he's old enough to go camping, he'll soon learn to carry what's needed.' He then showed me how to 'shoulder' the bag. Mother opened the hall door as father said 'away yea go then, have a great time'. 'Mind yourself son. Don't forget to say your prayers'. That was Mother.

So off I went, along Benbulbin Road to board the number 22 bus at Mourne Road, which would bring me to O'Connell Street. Getting off the bus in town, the bag was once again 'shouldered' and I walked to Aston's Quay where some of my fellow Cubs were already gathered. Mr Healy checked that we were all there and our bags were loaded on the bus for Tibradden. The journey out to the Dublin mountains wasn't all that unfamiliar to us as we had often hiked the route. In fact, a hike usually started from Rathfarnham which was a couple of miles further back. There was still a mile or so to go, so as soon as our entire luggage was off the bus we headed off in what was called 'Indian' file. Keeping to the right-hand side of the winding rural road, our single line of excited Cubs advanced on Larch Hill. It seemed as if additional items were being added to my pack because every ten minutes it felt heavier.

It was great to see the entrance gates of the national campsite, but the most difficult part of the walk was still ahead. Encouraged on by our leaders, light-heartedly calling out 'we're nearly there boys' we trudged the final half mile of rising, twisting road to the Cub Field. Finally I set my knapsack down against a barbed-wire sheep fence and felt a sense of achievement.

Immediately on arrival, each Six was allocated a tent and shown where to pitch it. 'In the nearest river' one cheeky Cub said. The older and more experienced Cubs removed the heavy tent from its valise and spread it out flat while those new to tent pitching were directed by the Sixer to assemble the main and ridge poles. With the poles in position on the canvas, the tent was raised. My job that day was to hold on to one of the poles and keep it vertical while others pulled on the guy ropes, spreading the canvas. Only the more senior Cubs were allowed drive the wooden pegs with what seemed to me at the time to be an enormous wooden mallet. Finally, the guy ropes were adjusted and the canvas became taut. Dermot Richardson inspected each tent and advised on any adjustments that were necessary to have the tent pitched perfectly. Part of each camper's equipment was a ground sheet and each one of us spread this out to cover the grass floor in our allotted tent.

The next task was to prepare our beds. The two woollen blankets now had to be fashioned into a sort of large envelope. The first was laid out flat on the ground and the second blanket overlapped this to the halfway point. The uncovered half of the first blanket was then folded back over the second, again to the half way point and finally the protruding half of the second was folded over the first. The large blanket pins pierced through the four folds along the two long sides and across one short side. A badly made bed meant an uncomfortable night as cold air would enter the bag through the seams. This would be the standard way to make a camp bed for many years until the commercial sleeping bag became available. Each bed was then rolled from the bottom towards the top and the rolls placed neatly along one wall inside the tent. It was important to have these tasks completed before nightfall and, no matter how tired or hungry you might be, the first task was to select a suitable site and set-up camp.

Around each tent, a low post and string fence defined the boundaries or territory for each Six. To erect this boundary it was necessary to go and find suitable wooden stakes in the forest. Great emphasis was placed on not damaging trees and so we looked for a fallen bough and trimmed the branches to make straight sticks about ninety centimetres long. These were driven into the ground two meters apart and four or five meters out from the tent on all four sides. Strong string, sisal, was attached to the top of the stakes from one to the other, leaving a gap opposite the door to the tent which was the entrance to our particular site.

While all this was going on, a couple of adult leaders had 'cut a sod' and prepared a cooking fire. Having arrived in Larch Hill at about 7 p.m., by the time the campsite was in good order it was becoming dark and a little chilly. We gathered around the crackling warm fire and from a steaming Billy Can we each had our mug filled with hot cocoa. As we sipped the steaming drinks, Mr Healy complimented us on the good job we had made of preparing camp and outlined the night rules. With the radiating heat of the fire on my face and the warmth from the cocoa I was really glad I had joined the Cub Scouts. Night prayers around the campfire were the final event for the day and we moved off towards our tents. Just before entering my tent for the night, I wandered over to the edge of the field and stood by a sheep fence and was fascinated by the twinkling lights of Dublin City way off in the distance and the canopy of stars in the sky overhead. I particularly remember the distinctive amber coloured streetlights which snaked along the Howth coast road to the north-east and perhaps over twenty miles away. I remember thinking that this was an experience not to be missed and I felt privileged to be there. After night prayers, we finally slid into our bedrolls and even after a hectic day, sleep was still a long way off. The older Cubs launched into ghost stories which were meant to 'put the frighteners' into us new recruits. Perhaps they succeeded or maybe it was the darkness and stillness of my first night in the mountains which kept me awake.

Larch Hill, the National Campsite at that time, had little or no amenities and next morning we washed in the cold waters of a nearby stream and, after breakfast, we were ready for a weekend of fun and adventure. Arriving home on Sunday evening after the most exciting weekend an eight year old could have, Mother unpacked my knapsack and was mystified to say the least as to how sausages became coated in tinned milk, sugar and tea leaves in the bottom of the bag. Of course I had no explanation for the mess and Father just remarked, 'he will soon learn'. He was correct, as usual.

Getting to and from the 'Den' in the winter time could at times be an adventure in itself. Inchicore Terrace had no street lighting or pavement and was bounded on both sides by very high stone walls, so a good few of us carried hand torches to light the way. Sometimes, on the journey home we were confronted by groups of local boys who would try to stop us passing along the road but our expertise in the game of 'bulldog' generally saw us through. On one dark night the locals had mustered reinforcements in the form of their big brothers. The extra numbers and taller boys made us reconsider the usual charge. A couple of runners were sent back to the Den and our numbers were increased with Scouts and Senior Scouts. The attack was organised and on the command 'charge' we easily overcame the local boys and reached the main road without any casualties.

I enjoyed every moment of the three years as a Cub Scout. In addition to the hiking and camping, and learning new skills I developed an interest in first aid. I had discovered a Fire Service first aid handbook belonging to my father and studied this with interest. Somehow Mr Healy became aware of my interest and encouraged me by instruction in the uses of the triangular bandage. I was further encouraged when he suggested I should be the bearer of the first-aid bag when we were on outdoor activities. Progressing through the ranks, I finally reached the dizzy heights of Senior Sixer. On reaching eleven years of age (the maximum for a Cub Scout) I transferred to the Scout section. Going from a position of seniority in one section to the lowliest in another was difficult for some to accept and often left Scouting at this point. For me, moving to the Scout section was something I really looked forward to, with the prospect of greater adventures and besides, I would get to wear the terrific looking 'mountie' hat.

3

THE SCOUTS

The unit had lost the use of their meeting place in 1950 and the patrols met in parents' homes, usually that of the Sixer in the case of the Cubs, or Patrol Leader for the Scouts. In some cases it was not practical to meet in private homes due to family circumstances and the Six or Patrol would meet under a street light. 'Pop' Downes and other leaders would then cycle around to meet each group to check on progress and keep everyone up to date on events. I belonged to the Lion Patrol and although I was only a lowly Scout, we met in Mammy's kitchen. As an ex-Scout, Dad knew that it was preferable if we had a space to call our own and suggested we use the garden shed. The Lion Patrol members were delighted and as a team we soon had all the junk cleared out and even painted the walls. With charts and pictures decorating the walls our new mini Den had a sense of permanency about it.

Some time later the unit was to get the use of a derelict building located in a place known as The Valley. Situated between the Naas Road near Bluebell and Kilworth Road, this disused farm building was adjacent the banks of the Cammock River. Getting to our new Den wasn't exactly straightforward. There was no established route and access to the valley was gained through a break between private houses a short distance along the Naas Road. At the back of these houses there was a gap in a high railing and passing through this brought us onto the slope of the valley. If the weather was fine and the evening bright, then the route was an easy enough one, but on a wet, dark night the going could be rough. Slipping and sliding our way to the Den meant many mud-covered uniforms and a lot of washing for the mammies. Given the fact that washing machines were practically unheard of, it was, I am sure, a chore they could have done without.

The building had been without doors on the ground floor for some time which gave free rein to the cattle from the surrounding fields. The ground floor was at least ankle deep in mud and cattle dung and so it could not be used initially. In one of the gable ends on the first floor there was a single door, so it was through this we gained access. For each meeting, a ladder was placed against the wall and we climbed up, one at a time until we were all assembled. As there was no electricity, the business of the meeting was conducted by the atmospheric glow of paraffin oil lamps. In time, the ground floor was cleaned up and we could play games, which helped to keep us warm on the cold nights. With all its drawbacks, it was better for the Patrols to meet as a troop rather than be spread about the parish.

It was a challenging time for the unit and great credit must go to the leaders of the time for holding the unit together in difficult circumstances.

In 1952, St Theresa's Unit would once again relocate. The Headquarters of the CBSI was located at the Earlsfort Terrace end of St Stephen's Green, number 71. To the rear of this fine Georgian building was a large garden. A building at the end of the garden had been used by the organisation's boxing club, but the club's activities had ceased and the building became vacant. Headquarters gave permission to the 35th to take up occupancy. Through disused there were some emergency repairs to be done and in October the new Den was blessed at a ceremony attended by senior officers of the CBSI.

Having a place to meet for the exclusive use of the unit meant a lot and with the help of willing volunteers the walls were brightly painted. The main room was where the boxing ring was originally located so there was ample room to allocate a space or 'Patrol corner' to each Patrol. Each space was personalised with individual patrol colours, emblems and charts.

It was around this time that the uniform shirt was changed from blue to grey. The new short-sleeved grey shirt was much lighter than the warmer long-sleeved original and although there were many debates over which was preferable, the grey light-weight won the day. The change also meant the end of a popular Scout song, some of the words were as follows, 'When you get a line on a new recruit, make him a Scout in the navy blue suit.' The other major change was replacing the distinctive Mountie hat with a black beret.

The building contained two other rooms. One was used as a store for camping equipment and the other as a small leaders' room complete with fire place. The former also contained rowing oars, ship's bell, lots of ropes and other marine bits and pieces. This equipment had been in use by the Sea Scout Section of the unit, the 9th Port, but the section was now defunct. The leaders' room was also the administrative centre; it contained the unit files and it was where activities were planned by the officers and Patrol Leaders. With comforts such as electricity and portable oil heaters, the nomadic period for the unit was well and truly at an end.

It was now possible to stage events to which parents, brothers, and sisters could be invited. As there was no dividing wall between the stores or Sea Scout room and the main room, this was an ideal location for a temporary stage to be constructed. With wings and backdrop made from canvas and as in most DIY efforts, the obligatory 'sticking curtains' the unit made its debut in show business. This winter activity was to become popular and was the forerunner to more semi-professional shows in the future. During one of these early shows, on a wet winter's night, the audience sat with raised umbrellas through part of the show, highlighting the need for funds to repair the roof. All sections of the unit made their contribution to the show and, as the audience was made up of parents and family, the cock-ups only added to the entertainment. One such act, 'The Blue Ray' went down a treat as the theatrical gun went off and shot the main character well before the appointed time. I think the best part for the parents was when the refreshments arrived. The luxuries of the Den did not extend to kitchen facilities so the Knight-Errant Clan built a fire in the garden. A twenty-gallon drum of water was boiled and several hiking socks (washed ones) full of loose tealeaves were suspended therein until the brew was ready. The cups of tea and biscuits which followed helped make these occasions a success.

As part of the personal development programme, the Unit Council instigated a craft competition. There was no obligation to take part but most did. Entries included drawing, painting, woodcarving and a popular one was fretwork. Like most boys I liked to assemble projects using Meccano and looked forward to Christmas when I would get the additional items supplied as a kit, which brought whatever kit number you had up to the next stage. The fret-saw and basic accessories which I received one Christmas developed my interest in working with wood. Design sheets could be bought in Healy's on Dame Street (long since gone) and appeared in hobby magazines. Pipe smoking was common and there were many designs to choose from. As father had several pipes I made the best pipe rack possible and I was pleased that he fixed it to the wall by the fire, where it stayed, full of pipes for many years.

Within a couple of years of learning to draw at George Colley's art school, I decided one year that my entry would be a watercolour. I chose to draw and paint a portrait of St Theresa, 'The Little Flower', as she was the patron saint of the unit. To my delight my entry won first prize. What surprised me was the prize: a really good quality sheath knife. Most senior Scouts carried one of these as part of uniform but certain tests had to be passed first. Known as 'knife and axe' it involved being aware of the uses for which the knife was intended and also the correct and safe method for its care and use. The same applied to the axe. Having won the prize and keen to wear it, it was not long before I had met all the requirements.

With no Scout Troop close to where I lived, many of the members of the Donore Avenue Troop came from around my area. Starting at the extreme south end of the parish, each Scout would set out on his bicycle and, *en route* towards the Den, meet up with others. By the time they reached my house, where I was waiting with my neighbour Frank Donnelly, the group usually consisted of Tom Murphy, Georgie Nolan and Bill and Brendan Lawlor. Travelling on down Galtymore Road we were joined by Liam Lawlor. There were others from our parish but not everyone had bicycles so some walked while others travelled by bus. During wet weather it was possible to get some protection from the rain by cycling close to the back of a bus. Besides the obvious danger of this tactic, the fact that tram tracks were still in place on the South Circular Road made the activity even more challenging. Because of the wet stone cobbles and steel rails many a front wheel slid into the tram track with the resulting flight over the handlebars.

There was no need to 'tail a bus', as we called it, in the summer time. However, occasionally, on the rear-boarding platform of a bus one would find one of Dublin's best known characters, 'Bang Bang'. We pedalled furiously as he fired at us with his famous big iron door key, with us returning fire just as enthusiastically. At some bus stops he would jump from the platform and run towards the front of the bus. Pointing his key at the driver's cab he would shout out, 'Bang Bang' and then make a hasty retreat and be back on board before the bus moved on to the next stop. Some drivers feigned death by slumping over the steering wheel which pleased him very much and amused the passengers.

4

ANNUAL CAMP

The highlight for any Scout Troop worth its salt has to be Annual Camp. It is a time for adventure, travelling to other parts of the country and overseas to experience other cultures. It is also a time to put into practice the skills acquired on training hikes and weekend camps. Potential sites were visited by two or three leaders to confirm what was on offer some months prior to the date set for camp. On the basis of site conditions and facilities as well as local attractions, a selection would then be made. Cost was given serious consideration so that no one was excluded.

A comprehensive list of the personal essentials necessary for the two weeks was issued to each Scout and was to be used when packing his haversack. Of great importance was the parent consent form, where details of special medical needs, if any, were recorded. So as not to cause any embarrassment, this information was of course confidential and known only to the leaders and in particular the Camp Medical Officer. Well in advance, a full programme of activities was planned and in the event of inclement weather, a wet-weather programme was drawn up for the full duration of the camp.

A few weeks before camp, each patrol carried out an inspection of their equipment to ensure no items were missing. Occasionally a Billy Can or two or a few tent pegs was lost during a weekend camp earlier in the year and now was a good time to make replacements. A tent or dining shelter might need repair and to discover this at the campsite was too late. It could be said that the excitement of Annual Camp began long before the 'off date' with all this necessary preparation. The foregoing is an outline of the preparations for Annual Camp, which has gone on in St Theresa's Unit for over eighty years and, please God, will continue for another eighty and more.

At age twelve, my first Annual Camp with the Scout section was to Greenane in County Wicklow. There is a lot of media coverage today regarding the inadequacies of our national transport infrastructure, but in 1951 it hardly existed at all. Private coaches were in use in some parts of the country but these were mainly used to bring people from local rural areas to town. Private cars were few and not an option for a group of forty or more as well as all the camping equipment. Liam Lawyer's dad provided a 'Turf' lorry and when all equipment was loaded we climbed aboard. Using tents and anything else soft as seats to smooth out the bumps in the road, we happily set out on the two-hour journey. Now and again, led by Kevin Grennan, the Assistant Scoutmaster, we sang the Scout songs we had learned during the year. This was a great help in shortening the journey and brought smiles to the faces of townspeople as a lorry load of singing boys passed through Bray, Rathnew and Wicklow. Finally we arrived at Ballinacor estate and our Scoutmaster Frank Geoghan and the Unit Leader Paddy (Pop) Downes and the rest of the leaders quickly organised us in setting up the camp site.

For the first couple of days we were kept busy putting the final touches to the site with boundary fences, wood piles and cooking fires. 'Pioneering' was the art of making washbasin stands, mug trees, plate racks and other useful kitchen furniture using various thicknesses of tree branches. Each branch was trimmed of twigs and cut to length to form a straight pole and joined to each other using strong string or sisal. We had practised square and diagonal lashings at troop meetings and now came the time to test our skills. With most of the essentials in place, there was more time for other activities such as swimming in the Avonbeg River, which was adjacent to the site, and playing games. Although we were always kept busy and had lots of fun it was not uncommon for one or two Scouts to become homesick after a week or so. This generally applied to someone away from family and home for the first time. Adult officers were trained to recognise the signs and, with the help of the Patrol Leaders, usually overcame the problem. In very exceptional circumstances, a Scout would be returned home accompanied by an officer. I'm glad to say this was not something I experienced and perhaps it was partly due to the fact that I had at this stage been camping with the Cubs for three years.

For an urban dweller, I have always enjoyed getting away to the countryside and, in particular, the mountains. I would describe the site in Greenan as magical and the wild surrounding terrain made a lasting impression on me. Bounded on the west by Lugnaquillia, at (926m/3,039ft.), the highest summit in Wicklow and to the north, Glenmalure at 2,179 feet high, to the south is Croaghanmoira and to the west is Rathdrum. There was one shop in Greenan which was also the local post office, grocer and public house. This was our 'tuck' shop and we were allowed go there a few times a week. The camp treasurer would give each of us the same amount of spending money from the camp bank, so we were all equal. This allowed us buy a bar of chocolate, a few sweets and perhaps an ice-cream. To send a postcard home to family, it might be necessary to forego the ice-cream. During the second week we dressed in full uniform and hiked the three miles to Rathdrum village where we spent what was left of our money on presents for parents and brothers and sisters. If there was anything left over it naturally went on 'goodies'.

The camp at Greenan made such an impression on me, that thirty years later I bought a site to the east side of the Avonbeg River and obtained planning permission to build a house but that's another storey.

The troop's preparations and planning for annual camp have remained much the same over the last eight decades, proving that the system handed down over such a long time works well. My next annual camp, in 1952 was to Stradbally in County Laois, quite close to where I now live. The campsite was situated on the Cosby estate and was an ideal location for outdoor pursuits. The Cosbys first came to Ireland in the middle of the sixteenth century and the estate of over 500 acres has remained in unbroken ownership by the family for fourteen generations. The first 100 years or more for the Cosby settlers were not easy, as the native Chieftains, mainly the O'Dwyers, engaged in many battles. For four generations the owners of the estate paid the ultimate price and it was only towards the end of the seventeenth century that real progress was made. Colonel Alexander Cosby erected a mill and other town buildings and the town of Stradbally began. Cosby Hall, the mansion at the estate is said to be the largest residence in the country. Successive generations have contributed to the development of the town and Adrian Cosby and his wife Allison continue this tradition to the present time. I was thirteen years of age when I first explored the town with my fellow Scouts and now, fifty years on, as I travel through Stradbally on my way to Carlow or Athy, the town's features remind me of those happy days.

In 1949, just before I transferred from the Cubs to the Scout section, my interest in first aid, which I have mentioned earlier, led me to join the St John Ambulance Brigade. I had no contacts in the organisation but some-how found out that meetings were held in a building on Strand Street, just off Capel Street. Some of the lectures covered subjects such as the uses of the triangular bandage or how to apply a splint which I had some knowledge of from Kevin Healy my Cubmaster, while other areas were new to me. A full-size adult skeleton, which we called 'Joey', stood at the top of the classroom and soon I was able to name all of his component parts. 'Tonight we will look at the bones, which make up the arm,' the lecturer would say and proceed to touch each bone of Joey with a pointing stick. As each name was called out, the class would echo the word. 'Humerus, Radius, Ulna' was repeatedly rhymed until it was impressed in our minds. Before long we knew Joey intimately. Armed with the principles of first aid, knowledge of the bones of the body and the practicalities of applying artificial respiration, I was ready for my first exam. With a certificate in Preliminary First Aid' signed on 1 December 1950 by the Commissioner and Examiner at Brigade Headquarters I was now ready for active service so to speak. But first I had to get a uniform. I'm sure, for my parents this was an expense they could have done without. They always encouraged my brothers and sisters, and myself in our activities, and I do not recall any occasion when some venture of ours was seen as too expensive to engage in. At some point my three sisters Pat, Frances and Mary were involved in the Girl Guides and taking private music and dancing lessons, while my brothers Jack and Bill were in Scouting. Fees and uniforms had to be paid for our varied activities for all six of us and must have been a strain on the purse strings.

I enjoyed donning the Cadet uniform for the first time. This consisted of black shoes, grey knee socks, black short pants and leather belt with shiny buckle. Above the waist consisted of a smart double-breasted grey tunic with chrome buttons and, for headgear, a black beret and chrome metal badge.

There was a feeling of anticipation as I boarded the number 22 bus for my first official duty in O'Connell Street. Being the main street in the capital city, it was a busy street for shoppers, tourists and visitors. Running

the length of O'Connell Street, the tree-lined walk-
way provided zones for parking bicycles, jaunting cars,
trams and taxis and at the base of the pillar hawkers who
traded fresh fruit. On this central pavement, opposite the
Gresham Hotel, the Brigade had a cream and black first
aid hut for the convenience of the public who might need
first aid treatment. As I crossed the road to the hut with
my white first aid bag bulging with bandages, plasters,
iodine, tweezers and scissors, I wondered would I really
be able to apply a splint to a broken leg or put an arm in a
sling. I need not have been concerned because anytime I
was on duty, the commonest injury was from people who
had got a bit of grit or dust in an eye. The most serious
case I had to treat was a cut hand, or to be more precise,
a scratched hand as a result of a fall. Nevertheless, after
washing and dressing the abrasion, I now felt my presence in O'Connel Street was justified and had a feeling of
intense satisfaction.

As my record of duties at the O'Connell Street post
grew, I began to get other assignments. One of the most
sought after were rugby matches at Lansdowne Road.
The game I remember best was between Ireland and the
All Blacks, which Ireland lost 14 – 3. Weekend activities
rotated between the St John Ambulance Brigade and
Scouting for a couple of years but these sometimes coincided with each other. As the number of dual engagements
increased, I knew I had to decide which one to stick with
and Scouting was my choice.

In 1953 Liam Bolger, Georgie Nolan and Richard Graham
and I became Patrol Leaders. Annual camp was to Dunmore

East in Waterford with Brendan Byrne as Scoutmaster and 'Pop' Downes as Camp Chief. From the campsite there was a panoramic view of the sea stretching out from the harbour. We walked daily to a small sandy beach close to the harbour and had great times swimming in the sea. The people of this small fishing village could not be friendlier and did everything they could to improve our stay. The lighthouse keeper arranged for us to visit and in small groups we climbed the spiral stairs. Patiently, he explained to each group how the lighthouse worked. It was amazing to see that the actual light was but a very small flame surrounded by specially arranged lenses. Revolving continuously around the flame the effect was to produce flashes at regular intervals which could be observed from a distance by ship crews at sea.

Can you imagine the excitement of young boys when told they were to go aboard a powerful motor lifeboat? This might be something a Sea Scout group would be more likely to arrange and even for them it would have been an experience to talk about. Down at the harbour we went aboard in patrol groups and listened to the skipper as he explained the characteristics of the vessel. 'By all accounts she is unsinkable,' he began, explaining that the many water-tight compartments ensured that even in the worst gales and high seas she would stay afloat. Even if the hugely powerful six-cylinder engines are under water, they will continue to work. Automatic valves throw out any water, which may enter. These and many more impressive statistics regarding the lifeboat were discussed among us for a few days. The lighthouse and lifeboat experiences were great but more was to come.

A trawler skipper offered to take the entire troop on board his boat. As Dunmore East was a major port for deep-sea and off-shore fishing there was therefore no shortage of trawlers. What we didn't know was that we were going to put to sea, until we heard the skipper call out, 'Cast off the stern line' and then 'Cast off the bow line'. As the engine revolutions increased, you could feel the vibrations through the deck and hear the thudding of the screw as it churned the water astern. Moving gently out through Waterford harbour we passed Hook Head and on out into St George's Channel. The initial excitement slowly abated as we became accustomed to the ship's fishy smell, the rolling movement and the throb of the engine. In high spirits I remember looking over the side and watching the foaming wash as it raced along the hull. Changing direction to the west brought about other changes as we approached the Atlantic Ocean. The height of the waves increased and at one point, on the crest of a wave, you could see the vast Atlantic as it stretched out to the horizon. Suddenly the bow seemed to drop and we were racing forward as if down the side of a mountain. We were now in a valley with mountains of water all around. No one onboard, except the crew of course, had experienced anything like it previously. At the bottom of the wave, it was as if someone had slapped on the brakes as the bow dug into the towering face of the next wave, the decks and all aboard were covered in sea spray. Initially at each wetting a resounding 'Yahoo' went up, and the boat slowly climbed to the next pinnacle. As the novelty of this new experience wore off, the excited cry changed to expletives which the leaders told us were inappropriate. Finally, back in port, forty very wet but exhilarated boys came ashore. The experience was one not to be missed but I think all decided to remain 'land lubbers'.

The next year, 1954, the unit celebrated its twenty-fifth year. Up to this time it had always been accepted that the 35th was founded in 1929. Information from Nicky Donegan, whom I referred to earlier, confirms that he joined the troop in April 1928, which means that the anniversary should really have taken place in 1953. Nevertheless it was that the celebrations got under way in February 1954 with a special Mass. This was followed by a Gala Parents Night, Handcraft Exhibition and a troop birthday party.

In 1955, the troop thought about going overseas and plans were put in place. Tawd Vale in Liverpool was chosen but I was not in a position to go as I had joined the Technical Training Squadron of the Irish Air Corps that year. The camp was a great success and I heard later that I would have enjoyed it because close to the campsite, an RAF squadron was based and performed aerobatics daily.

At this stage I was promoted to SPL (Senior Patrol Leader) and had also taken on the roll of troop Bugler from Bill Lawlor. The SPL, like the sergeant major in the army, was the link between the other ranks and officers. As such, I quartered with the leaders and it usually fell to Pop Downes to nudge me out of my sleep and say, 'Archie, time to blow reveille'. While the leaders slumbered in their warm sleeping bags I had to crawl out onto the damp dew-covered grass and taking hold of the cold metal of the bugle, blast everyone into a state of awakening. This was not an act that gained much popularity for me. I didn't realise until two decades later that Scouts at that time wanted to, 'do that bugler'. I was attending a Scouting event on the north side of the city and after the event a leader came up to me and said, 'You're Archie Raeside, the bugler.' I said that I was. He then told me, that as a young lad he remembered wakening to the sound of a bugle and everyone in his tent saying, 'Who's blowing that feckin' bugle?' I think that was a compliment. As not too many troops had buglers, my services were usually called on at regional camps.

On regional camps there could be 200 or more Scouts, made up from six or seven troops from different parishes. Each troop competed against each other in various camp crafts and Scouting skills for the coveted regional trophy. The competition was intense, as the winner went on to represent their troop in the national competition, 'The Melvin'. In addition to the Scouting events, there was usually what was known as a 'wide' game called 'Capture the Flag'. Divided into two armies, the Blues and the Reds, each side could have 100 players or more. The object of the game was to capture the flag of the opposing 'army'. Members of each army were identified by a red or blue arm band and in the battle for the flag it was essential to capture as many of the enemies' arm bands as possible. If neither flag was captured within the prescribed time, the side with the most enemy armbands was declared the victor.

The base camps for each army could be a mile or more apart with woods and perhaps a river between them. To prepare a strategy for capturing the flag of the opposing side, the bases had first to be located. Spies were sent out to this end and had to report back within a given time period with possible locations. With each side engaged in similar exercises, these reconnaissance patrols attempted to remain unobserved, for if caught it would mean an early end to the game for some. With great stealth, hedges, ditches, trees and long grass were used as cover as each small group attempted to remain concealed as they moved forward. On one of these intelligence-gathering forays I attempted to camouflage myself using fern plants. The first couple came out of the ground by the root easily. In pulling the next one, my hand slid up the stem and cut deep into the index finger of my left hand. To this day I bear the scar as a reminder of my folly.

With the objective located, strategic plans were drawn up for the defence of our own flag and the capture of the enemy's. When patrols of opposing sides met, the 'rough and tumble' that ensued could be, and generally was, quite physical.

5

THE KNIGHT ERRANT CLAN

While living and studying with the Air Corps at Baldonnel, my Scouting activity was confined to weekends. With nine others of my own age I became a member of the newly formed Knight Errant Clan. The programme for this elite group was devised to cater for the over 15s or over 16s. The Clan was instrumental in maintaining an interest in Scouting for those who had outgrown the age group for which the core Scouting pro-gramme was devised.

It would also be the nucleus from which future leaders would be recruited. The more adult serving leaders were also members of the Clan. Jacky McNally, a dedicated and much respected Scout Leader was the Clan Chief. Hiking took on a more gruelling aspect and endurance hikes in the Dublin and Wicklow Mountains became a regular activity. Hikes continued throughout all seasons irrespective of the weather. We knew one of the popular outings as the

'Lug Ridge Walk'. I remember the height of Lugnaquilla because the figures correspond to my birthday: 3,039 feet (03-03-39). Sally Gap and the Wicklow Gap were familiar territories and included peaks such as Kippure and Djouce mountains. Winter hikes were my favourite, perhaps because I enjoyed the crunching sound of the frozen snow underfoot. Sometimes the mountain heather was blanketed in frozen snow and progress was slow as the first in line probed for a firm footing. Deviating from the established line sometimes resulted in a disappearing act when a soft spot was traversed.

As my desire to experience new adventures grew, I came up with the idea of climbing Ben Nevis in Scotland which would also give me an opportunity to meet Scottish family members for the first time. The apprentice school closed for the summer break during the first two weeks in August so I began making plans a couple of months earlier.

Taking note of what I had learned about trekking in mountain terrain, my first priority was to find a companion to accompany me on the adventure. My cousin Stephen McKeown and I were good mates and he enthusiastically agreed to take part. Every weekend from the middle of June to the beginning of August we met to prepare for what lay ahead: camping, swimming, running and endurance walks.

On one extremely windy day we were running along the beach at Portmarnock and noticed, some distance ahead, what we initially thought was a football being blown towards us. We stopped running and prepared to intercept the approaching object, which in fact turned out to be a hen. We caught the distraught hen and moved inland to the dunes. We searched the area for about a mile in search of a house which she might have come from. Our search was in vain, so we took her back to the comfort of our tent. She was visibly frightened and traumatised but after a while began to relax as she pecked at the breadcrumbs scattered on the grassy floor of the tent. As our new-found feathered friend settled down we decided to make a cup of tea before breaking camp. The 'whoff' of the flame igniting on the portable Primus stove startled the hen and as she leapt over the stove her tail feathers were singed.

When it was time to leave we agreed not to abandon her and had by now christened her 'Skinny'. How to provide some degree of comfort for a hen, travelling on a motorbike was the next consideration. The answer was to empty one of our backpacks and strap everything on top of the petrol tank, giving us an empty bag for the hen. She cackled a little when placed in the bag but soon settled down when the flap was secured. We were almost home, but near Victoria Quay we encountered very heavy rain and took shelter under the canopy at Heuston station. Stephen took the bag off his back and placed it at his feet. After a little while Skinny began to cackle. There were others who had taken shelter out of the rain and we noticed they were beginning to cast suspicious looks in our direction. Stephen, who was good at making bird sounds, repeated every cackle the hen made. The theory was that the observers would believe it was he who was making all the sounds. I'm not sure which was worse: the idea that I was travelling with a lunatic or the more obvious suggestion that we had stolen a hen from some chicken farm. We were relieved when the rain eased and we continued on our way unchallenged. A great fuss was made of Skinny when we took her out of the bag at Stephen's house. She became a pet in the McKeown household, even taking a place by the fireside of a winter's evening.

On a wet and windy August Saturday evening, Stephen and I went aboard the boat bound for Glasgow. Unlike the modern car ferries, the ships crossing the Irish Sea in the 1950s transported cattle as well as people and the comforts were minimal. The experienced and more frequent travellers quickly filled what space was allocated to passengers. In fair weather it was preferable to remain on deck rather than endure the discomfort of the packed smoke-filled confines of the below deck areas. A good proportion of the passengers were crossing the Irish Sea from Dublin out of necessity, in search of work, or returning to their family for a short but well-earned holiday. Because of the inclement weather we went below and found a space in one of the corridors between the sleeping cabins. I remember thinking at the time, that if any of the passengers in the cabins needed to use the bathroom during the night, they would have to negotiate their way along a corridor of wall-to-wall people. In the knowledge that the journey would take as long as sixteen hours and assuming no one had a bladder with the capacity to hold out that long, at the first sign of daybreak Stephen and I were up on deck.

The ship docked at about 10 a.m. the next morning and an hour later we attended Mass in Glasgow. The next task was to locate Cumlodden Drive in Maryhill where Uncle Doddy lived. Except for my father's brothers and sisters, who had come to settle in Ireland with my grandmother in 1929, this would be my first contact with my extended family in Scotland. Donald Douglas (Doddy) made us very welcome and we spent the rest of the day catching up on family news. We stayed in his house for the night and next morning he took us to Aunt Sarah where I also met my cousin Archie Douglas. It struck me as strange that in seventeen years there had been no physical contact with my father's siblings. Now, older and I think wiser, I know this was not uncommon on both sides of the Irish Sea at that time. After a cup of tea and a chat, I took a few photographs with me and we bade farewell to my new-found family acquaintances and began our journey north.

We hiked out of Glasgow for seventeen miles before hitching a lift to Inverbeg. We pitched the tent at Glen Douglas for the night having completed the first thirty-two miles of the journey. Sleep did not come easy, as it was a particularly cold night, so we were up early the next morning. After breakfast we hiked on through Tarbet on the west bank of Loch Lomond. The miles slipped easily away as we admired the rugged splendour of the mountains which contrasted with the great expanse of water. I was very impressed with the ever-changing scenic beauty of the twenty-mile long Loch and its many islands, which seemed to float on the surface of the water. As well as discussing the possibility of a sighting of 'Nessie', we sang what we knew of the well-known song about the loch:

By yon bonnie banks, and by yon bonnie braes,
Where the sun shines bright, on Loch Lomond,
Oh we two have passed, so many blithesome days,
On the bonnie, bonnie banks o' Loch Lomond.

1 Hiking in the Dublin Mountains, 1951. Scout Leaders Kevin Grennan and Frank Gaeghan at the rear. Author in front row, third from left.

2 Annual Camp, 1953, at Dunmore East. Camp chief Paddy Downes in thoughtful mode, hand on tent. Author (wearing beret).

3 Author and younger brother John.

4 Taking a break. Work party at Larch Hill, 1956.

5 New-born lambs are rescued by Kevin O'Reilly and Paul Kenny.

6 President Eamon de Velera and escort arriving at Larch Hill, 1972.

7 President Eamon De Valera enters the new Training Centre.

8 The colour party representing many Scout Troops at the new building.

9 The author's sons, Cub Scouts Martin and Eugene, with Bernie in 1973.

10 Catherine (daughter of the author) with her Captain, Joan Farrell.

11 The author meets up with local scout group in Kivu in the Congo.

12 'Tuning-up' with the Merchant's Quay Scout Pipe Band. The author (bearded) is on the right and his brother Bill is on the left.

13 Cub Scouts blow out the candles on the 50th Anniversary Cake. Holding the cake,
author and Paddy Commerford.

VISIT OF POPE JOHN PAUL II
PHOENIX PARK
ZONE A
NAME: ARCHIE RAYSIDE
TITLE: 11 BENBULLEN ROAD
ADDRESS: DUBLIN 12.

14 Author's identity card for Papal visit.

15 Cub Scouts meet for a hike in 1982. Archie Jnr is at the front, looking at the camera.

Oh ye'll take the high road and I'll take the low road,
An I'll be in Scotland before ye',
But woe is my heart until we meet again
On the bonnie, bonnie banks o' Loch Lomond.

I mind where we parted, in yon shady glen
On the steep, steep side o' Ben Lomond
Where in purple hue, the highland hills we view
And the morn shines out Frae the gloaming.

Chorus
The wee bird may sing, an' the wild flowers spring;
An' in sunshine the waters are sleeping
But the broken heart, it sees nae second spring,
And the world does na ken how were grieving.

On hearing this song as a young lad at practically every party in our house, it never occurred to me that it was a sad love song when I joined in with gusto.

Private car ownership was very low in the mid-1950s which meant that there could be more hiking than hitching at times, leaving much time for singing or talking. What motorists there were at the time tended to be generous when it came to giving a hiker a lift. At the north end of the loch we were lucky to have a motorist take us on the remaining thirty or so miles to Glencoe.

Youth hostels were very popular among hikers and hill walkers. It was the least expensive form of overnight accommodation and, unlike a hotel or B&B, arriving in hiking attire was acceptable. Although my preference was for camping out, I joined An Oige so as to have a back-up plan for over-nighting. It was at Glencoe that I stayed at one of these hostels for the first time. It was a pleasant experience: meeting and talking to people with like mind around a log fire that night. Before leaving the hostel next morning, each visitor was expected to complete some chore. My task was to fill a couple of buckets with coal and leave them next to the range.

Having had a comfortable night and with a hearty breakfast inside us, we set out for the ferry at the west end of Loch Leven. When the raft-type ferry deposited us on the north bank of the loch, we were within twelve miles of Fortwilliam. Anxious to establish base camp, we proceeded on through the town and followed the river south east for a few miles along Glen Nevis. Having selected a tranquil spot by a bend in the river we pitched the tent and cooked a meal. After resting for an hour or two we walked back into Fortwilliam to have a look around the town.

The next morning we were in no hurry to cast off the blankets as we were advised not to attempt the climb early because of the likelihood of mist or fog on the mountain. Upon rising, my first action was to enjoy a swim in the clear, cool water of the mountain river. This put me in good form for a plate of hot porridge followed by fried sausages and bread and butter. In the early afternoon, following another swim, we began the climb. Except for one particularly steep and shaley slope, the accent was not particularly arduous, similar in many ways to climbing in the Wicklow mountains. We reached the 4,406ft peak without too much effort. Although there was a slight haze to the west, the view was spectacular and definitely worth the climb. Back at our riverside base, we brewed a Billy Can of tea and reminisced on the adventure. Stephen and I were content that we had accomplished our objective, of standing on the highest mountain in the British Isles.

Except for a lift on the back of a Bedford lorry for about ten miles, we made the return journey to Glasgow on foot over the next two days. Back in Glasgow we had a further two days to explore the city, visit some art galleries and go to the cinema.

The trip remains a memorable one for a number of reasons. It was my first time on holiday outside Ireland, meeting some of my extended family in Scotland was a pleasure, and climbing Ben Nevis was very satisfying. With a sense of fulfilment I was able to enthusiastically apply myself to my studies at Baldonnel for the rest of the year. The following year was a busy one and Scouting took second place to studies, motorcycling and girls.

The Knight Errant Clan continued to be active and in 1958 it was decided to introduce a kilt as part of their uniform. The Leinster Plaid (tartan) was adopted as the most appropriate design. Not surprisingly, the question 'What's worn under the kilt?' was asked on more than one occasion. Usually with a smile on the face of the enquirer, I had heard this question put to my father many times. As a Scot, his reply was either 'myself' or, 'There's nothing worn; it's all in good order'. As far as I know, none of the Clan members had the courage to adopt the wearing of the kilt in its purist arrangement.

Official sanction from the National Executive Board was not sought for this radical change in uniform dress. The first official public wearing of the kilt took place at the inauguration of the 82nd Dublin Scout unit in Drimnagh. Liam Bolger and Georgie Nolan, two members of our unit had transferred to the new unit as leaders, which helped to cement a strong bond between the two units. The founding of a new unit is always a special occasion and we were aware that officials from National Headquarters would be present. There was a little apprehension as to what reaction there might be and we even considered that there might be moves to oppose the change. Our unit assembled at my parents' home, which was used as a location to store overcoats and, after forming up, we paraded to the parish church. The only official reaction to the new kilts was one of bemused disbelief, so the kilt became an accepted part of uniform for the 35th Dublin Knight Errant Clan.

In 1958, the Annual Camp was held in Chirk in North Wales. Paddy Commerford and myself were unable to travel with the troop but together we made the journey a few days later. The hospitality of the people of Chirk is particularly memorable and many friendships developed. Almost every night we formed a circle around a fire and sang many of our popular troop songs. Like the Irish, the Welsh are renowned for their singing prowess and visitors regularly joined the campfire circle. On one occasion the local Scout Troop and Guide Company joined in. Lord Trevor, the owner of the estate came to the campsite on many evenings, to share a cup of cocoa and join in the campfire. For the closing campfire at the end of the two weeks, the job of producing posters advertising the event fell to me. These were displayed locally and received a good response. In addition to the local people, the attendance included a group of Irish road-workers that were delighted to contribute to the renditions.

Paul Kenny, one of my many Scouting friends, had his leg broken while playing cricket. He was treated in hospital and it seemed he would have to stay on in Chirk after the troop returned to Ireland. The local people became aware of the situation and they offered to bring Paul's parents to Wales and provide accommodation for them. Fortunately, aided by crutches, he was able to travel with the troop and the exceptional generosity of the people of Chirk to assist was not called into play.

At this time, the Knight Errant programme was having varying degrees of success within the association. Many Clan members were in their early twenties and as a result, interests and lifestyles were changing. Most had embarked on careers and for some their social activities now included dancing and girls. For the fifteen- and sixteen-year-olds, leaving mainstream Scouting, the programme required a new approach to maintain their interest. I believed the programme needed to embrace a much wider variety of activities in order to appeal to potential new members. My ideas were seen as too radical and outside the traditional Scouting ethos and perhaps not within the constraints of the constitution.

Not wishing to rock the boat, I decided to test my ideas outside the restrictions of the National body. Two of my friends, Ian O'Reilly and David Brennan, were enthusiastic about the project and agreed to support it. We started by renting a cottage at Lady's Lane in Kilmainham. As soon as we had the two rooms painted and decorated we began recruiting members. My brothers Jack, who was fifteen years of age and Bill who was thirteen, put the word out and soon six of their friends joined the group. We now had the first 'Patrol' in place and training started immediately. An identity was needed so after some discussion the great adventurer St Brendan was adopted as our icon and we became known as St Brendan's Rover Scouts.

Taking note of the interests of each member we gave encouragement for each to pursue his particular favourite subject and helped as far as we could. The traditional Scouting skills and activities formed a large part of our meeting and outings. In addition we included music, art, model making and nautical and aviation related activities. Within a few months, as numbers grew, we moved to a nearby cottage which had an extra room.

The experiment was going well and in July 1960 I was selected by Military Headquarters to accompany the first Irish United Nations Peacekeepers to serve in the Congo as their official photographer. Letters and photographs from Ian and David kept me informed about the activities while I was away. As related in an earlier book about my experiences in the Congo, I made contact with Scout units wherever I went. There is a unity of purpose within the Scouting movement world-wide and we had much to share. When I returned from Africa in 1961 the other leaders and myself did not have the time to remain actively involved and so the section was disbanded. There was never any intention to set up an alternative to the long-established Scouting movement. The objective was to test an approach, which could provide young people with the opportunity to pursue and perfect existing skills and develop an interest in new activities.

6

NATIONAL REVAMP

Mainstream Scouting would in time introduce water and air activities. The Knight Errant programme would end, being replaced in 1961 with a Venture Programme for the over fifteen year olds.

Meanwhile, those at the helm at national level had come to realise that it was time for change and recognised that a new approach was called for to cater to the needs of young people. Two hundred leaders from all the provinces met in the Shelbourne Hotel in March 1962. It was the first such gathering and its purpose was the introduction of a new system of test work and the beginning of revisions in programme activities.

Between the end of the Knight Errant era and the start up of the Venture Programme, an attempt to cater for the over fifteens was activated. The members of this group were to be known as 'Seniors'. Due to heavy commitments with the Air Corps at Gormanstown Air Base in 1961, and the fact that Bernie and I married in April 1962, my involvement with Scouting was limited but, with Kevin Healy, I did become involved in the Senior Scouting experiment and continued to attend Unit Council meetings.

In my experience as a Scout Leader, this age group should call the shots to some extent but adult involvements are essential to co-ordinate and guide them in their decisions. Most of the new group had entered Scouting at age eight as Cub Scouts and so were very familiar with hiking, camping, fire lighting, cooking and other skills. We encouraged the group to set new challenges for themselves utilising these skills and also to consider new areas of interest. Subject possibilities were wide ranging and we helped source the required information to the satisfaction of the group.

The National Headquarters building at 71 Stephen's Green was sold in 1962 and the new National Headquarters was located at 19 Herbert Place; as a result St Theresa's Unit was once again without a meeting place. Resulting from a newspaper advertisement, a private garage in Arbutus Avenue near Sally's Bridge was acquired. From this less than ideal accommodation, the unit flourished over the next five years and traditional Scouting skills continued to develop under the leadership of Paddy Downes, Paddy Commerford, Tommy Whelan, Paddy Sullivan, Brendan Holohan, Jimmy Austin, Ciaran Doherty, Sean Darcy and Tommy Hartnett.

Annual Camps during these years took place in Aughengillen in Scotland, Glenstall Abbey in Limerick, Cahir, Buckmore Park near London and Jersey.

It became increasingly obvious that the existing facilities for meetings of all sections of the unit were inadequate and the Unit Council decided something had to be done about it. Following discussions with the owner of the rented premises it was agreed to lease some of the adjoining land in order to extend the building. Fundraising got under way in the form of a lottery, which was called 'The Silver Circle'. All members of the unit and their families and friends supported the project on a weekly basis and work soon started. The funds were not sufficient to employ a contractor so all the work was undertaken by volunteers on evenings and at weekends. The greatly improved facility was ready for the unit's fortieth birthday celebrations in 1969.

For any voluntary organisation, fundraising requires considerable effort in planning and implementation. At national level, a sponsored walk was organised and called the 'Big Big Charity Walk' and took place on Sunday 18 May 1969. It was one of the first events of this type to take place in Ireland and in the following years many other organisations saw the potential for this type of fundraising. This particular walk was over a distance of twenty miles. First Aid stations were set up every few miles and many availed of these to have blistered feet and strained muscles attended to. Fresh drinking water was also provided. The distance for most charity walks in the years that followed tended to be over a distance of ten miles or twenty kilometres.

In the late 1960s, a commission was established at national level to make recommendations for new guidelines for Scouting which the National Council at a number of meetings then studied. Finally, on 1 January 1970, a new constitution was adopted. Changes to badge requirements for rawly and second class tests were introduced. Another development of the late 1960s and early '70s was the introduction of female leaders to the Cub section of the association and Una Kelly became the first female to join the 35th as Assistant Cub Leader.

In 1971, the troop undertook its first continental trip, travelling to Le Havre in France and visited the birth place of the unit's patron saint, St Theresa. The Cubs annual camp was to the newly opened hostel at Larch Hill. One of the troop's strong points has always been campfire singing and in 1972 they won the area campfire competition and came third in the diocesan competition.

On the 4 June the same year, the official opening of the new Larch Hill centre took place. As I drove to the venue with my father that afternoon I was stopped by a Garda about a mile from the entrance. He told me the road was closed to all traffic because the President Eamon de Valera was due any moment. I asked if he could contact P.J. Killackey on his radio at the control centre for clearance, and to my surprise he complied and I was allowed drive on. On arrival at the main gate, I noticed a guard of honour of Scouts was formed up on both sides of the long driveway. The Scouts must have been briefed that the next car through would be that of the President, because as soon as I drove through the gates, long lines of Scouts came to attention and saluted smartly. The ritual repeated as we proceeded along the driveway, all the way to the house. I guess Dad was amused at apparently been mistaken for the President of Ireland.

He took many photographs on the day including the arrival of the real Presidential car and close ups of the chief. The Archbishop of Dublin, Most Revd Dr Dermot Ryan performed the official blessing of the centre prior to concelebrated Mass. Speakers on the day were Mr Michael O'Kennedy TD, Dr Laszlo Nagy Secretary General Boy Scouts World Bureau, and Mr Stephen Spain Chief's Scouts Deputy CBSI.

My sons Eugene and Martin joined the Unit as Cub Scouts in 1973 and so began the third generation of Raesides' to be involved in Scouting. As mentioned in my opening paragraphs, Dad was involved in Scouting in Scotland and continued to be supportive. At this time, he was assisting Paddy Sullivan in compiling a photo-graphic record of the unit's history. Paddy put the word out and old photographs taken by parents, past mem-bers, leaders and friends began to surface. The owners of these pictures were promised that the originals would be returned so Dad photographed and printed them for Paddy's library. With the advent of digital photography, computers, and high-resolution copying, reproducing a photograph is now a simple matter but not so in the 1970s. It required a good quality camera with close-up lens and dark room facilities to develop the film and print the pictures, all of which Dad had, as he was a keen photographer.

Pop Downes decided it was time to organise the Seniors into a Venture Group. Leaders and committee members supported him and I accepted the role of Venture Leader. Under the leadership of Michael O'Donnell, the troop travelled to De Kluis in Belgium for annual camp. It was the first time for the troop to travel to camp by air and the first time to fly for the majority of the Scouts.

This was the year Fr Liam Bolger died. Liam and I served together as Patrol Leaders and as Knight Errants and I and all who had known him sorely felt his passing. As mentioned earlier, Liam was a founder leader with the 82nd Drimnagh Scout Unit. Liam's priestly title was Padre Guilherme Bolger CSSP and he was ordained on 2 July 1967. He served on the missions in Brazil from 1968 to 1972 and during that time maintained contact with his Scouting friends.

On 15 August the following year, Paddy (Pop) Downes died. He was a leader with the Unit for over thirty years, twenty-five of those as Unit Leader. He was respected by several generations of leaders for his dedication to the 35th and to Scouting in general. His ability to lead and influence others in all things Scouting was remarkable. At Mount Gerome Cemetery, a lone piper led the cortege to the graveside. I was honoured to be asked to sound a last tribute on the trumpet at the funeral. A commemoration Mass was held the following November in Donore Avenue and in excess of 700 Scouts from the region attended.

Prior to Pop's death, a decision was taken to retire the Unit flag (see Chapter 2) which had been in service for forty-two years and have a new flag made. Pop maintained the view that it should be ceremoniously burned. However, because of the history of the original flag and being the work of art that it was, the general consensus was that it would be framed and hung in a prominent position in the Den. The old flag was dispatched for framing and I was nominated to come up with a design for the new flag. The person with the job of having the old flag framed left his car in to have a minor petrol pump fault remedied and during the course of the work the car caught fire. The flag was in the boot together with some shotgun cartridges and a bottle of propane gas. The car along with three others, the garage and of course the beloved flag were burned to ashes. To this day, those of us who knew Pop believe he got his way.

The mantle of Unit Leader passed to Paddy Sullivan in 1975. He restyled the Unit Council to include representatives of parents as well as section leaders and the chaplain. Other highlights that year were the founding of a past members association chaired by Jack McNally and Jimmy McGovern as secretary and a tree planting ceremony at Larch Hill in memory of Pop Downes. This consists of a grove of thirty-five trees situated immediately inside the entrance to the National Campsite and Headquarters. The 1970s were a time of expansion at unit and national level, not just numerically but also in development and confidence. It was a time of growing ties and greater co-operation between the Catholic Boy Scouts of Ireland, the Scout Association of Ireland and the Northern Ireland Scout Council. The tri-partite conferences held at that time must surely be the forerunner to Scouting Ireland as it is today in the twenty-first century. I recall attending a very successful weekend Scout Leaders conference in Tramore in October 1975 and coming away with the feeling that there was a great future for Scouting in Ireland.

My son Eugene, my brother Bill and I joined the Scout Pipe Band at this time. I had been a founder member of the Air Corps Pipe Band but my initial training was cut short when I was posted to Africa so now I had a second chance to become a piper. Eugene had previous experience as a drummer with the Artane Boys Band and was therefore of immediate benefit to the band. By March of the following year we were proficient enough to walk with the band along O'Connell Street in Dublin for the St Patrick's Day parade.

My daughter Catherine joined the Girl Guides at this time. She travelled to the meetings and activities with our immediate neighbour Joan Farrell who was the Captain with the Inchicore group.

The organisation celebrated its golden jubilee in July and August 1977. A special camp called 'Jamborora '77' was in the planning for a couple of years previous and when it came to fruition there were some 12,000 participants from twenty countries taking part. The event took place in the grounds of the Cistercian Abbey of Mount Melleray in glorious weather. The success of the camp was due in no small measure to the leaders and Venturers from many units, including the 35th that provided work parties prior to the camp. Members of the unit also played a prominent part in the staffing of the camp. I was not actively involved but enjoyed a visit to the event and with Colm, Eddy, Brendan and Eugene from the pipe band and we enjoyed playing a few tunes.

All sections of the unit were flourishing at this time. Tommy Hartnett, having completed many years as leader of the Cub Pack handed over to Brenda Kenan with Gillian Roach, Kevin Cleary and Alan Fitzpatrick as assistants. Eamon Bolton took over from Frank Ryan as Venture Leader and the group took part in many exciting activities including orienteering, canoeing, horse riding and the Venture Challenge Shield.

The following year the troop won the National Cooking Competition, which included over one hundred teams from all the Scout and Guide organisations in Ireland. They also won the Regional Shield for the first time.

7

FIFTIETH ANNIVERSARY

For the fiftieth anniversary of the unit, it was decided to begin the celebrations by organising a weekend camp involving Cubs, Scouts, Venturers, parents and past members. On Friday 30 June 1978, Councillor Brendan Lynch attended a formal opening of the event at the Paddy Downes plot in Larch Hill. Following the formal opening the activities began in true Scouting fashion. Teams were formed from all the participating groups, from Cubs to past members, and competed against each other in a variety of challenges over the weekend. On the Saturday night, everyone gathered around a blazing campfire and as young and not so young sang with spirit there was a great sense of togetherness. Minister for State, Tom Fitzpatrick TD closed what was a very successful event on Sunday evening.

In addition to commitments to the Unit Council and past members and playing trumpet at various regional and other ceremonies, I accepted the role of Assistant Regional Commissioner for Venturers on an interim basis.

Celebrations continued on into the following year beginning with a dance on 9 February for adult members and friends of the unit and the following night a disco for Scouts, Venturers and their girlfriends in the Den. The weekend events came to a close with a special church parade in Donore Avenue church on Sunday. The chief Scout Joe Lawlor and the regional commissioner Brendan O'Brien attended this. The chief spoke of the unit's long history and of its many achievements and then presented long service medals to Paddy Commerford, Kevin Healy, Paddy Sullivan and myself.

In April, Paddy Commerford, Paddy Sullivan and Una and John Lawlor and I attended the National Council meeting in Sligo and stayed overnight in the Railway Inn.

My third son Archie joined the Unit on 10 May as a Cub Scout. At the end of the month the unit held a very successful fundraising event in the form of a 'fair' in the Donore Avenue school grounds.

One of the most momentous occasions for the country and for the association was the visit of Pope John Paul II on Sunday 29 September 1979. Preparations for the visit began some months earlier at Drogheda, Maynooth, Dublin, Knock, Galway and Limerick. Large numbers were involved prior to and during the visit in matters such as construction, traffic control, security, communications, public relations, first aid, transport, catering, marshalling and other functions. It attracted the largest number of participants in recent Irish history at the various venues around the country. At the Phoenix Park in Dublin there was well in excess of 1 million people. At the time I was working as in-house architect for John Sisk & Son and can recall the buzz in the office as large quantities of vital materials were being secured at short notice.

The 35,000 people involved in Scouting in Ireland played a significant part in helping to make the visit the success it was. Their tasks included forming human walls to help keep crowds back at various venues as well as acting as couriers and in general administrative duties. The Venturers were on duty from early morning, distributing tickets to everyone who streamed through the gates. My job was to form a team of six leaders to marshal the altar area zone A at the Phoenix Park. My team members included Paddy Commerford, Michael Morrissy, Frank Lawlor, Jimmy Attwell and Eugene Murphy. The first task, prior to the appointed day was to send the list with two passport-size photographs of each member to Garda headquarters for security reasons and to obtain a special identification card. Officially the gates opened to the public at 5 a.m. so I decided to be at my station before 4 a.m. Because of the early start, Paddy Commerford stayed overnight in my house and we set out for the park in my Mercedes at 3.30 a.m. Even at this early hour, as I drove through the Conningham Road entrance there was a lot of activity. Having found the allocated car-parking area 'H' we then proceeded to the altar.

Being close to my home, the Phoenix Park was a place where I enjoyed many a pleasant walk, played football and hurling, flew control-line and radio controlled model aircraft, and enjoyed the excitement of motor racing as a spectator. It was a new experience to arrive here in the hours of darkness and see the headlights of convoys of cars cut through the inky blackness as they slowly and quietly moved towards their allocated parking areas. The elevated altar was floodlit and the 116ft steel white cross could be seen for miles, glowing in the dark as the light reflected off it. As dawn approached, the golden rays of the rising sun produced a warm glow over the ceremonial hill. A sacristy and changing area was provided within the vault, which I got to view. The surface of the hill (now grassed), was stepped for access to the summit and the altar. From this vantage point I was amazed at the vast area which had been organised into large roped-off corrals for the public. From 5am thousands of people entered the park from various entrances. Prepared for a long wait, most brought a folding canvas deck chair and packed lunch. Sixty banners backed this centrepiece, each eighteen meters high and designed by Patrick Scott. His design was a papal coat of arms in the lower half topped with a yellow chevron pattern.

By 9.30 a.m. hundreds of thousands were assembled and shortly after, the Pope's aircraft flew over the park *en route* for Dublin airport. Four Irish Air Corps Fouga Magister jet aircraft of Light Strike Squadron escorted the Aer Lingus 747, *Saint Patrick* and when the formation came into view a great cheer went up from the excited masses. The 747, flown by Tom McKeown, carried on to land at Dublin and as the Pope disembarked, five Fouga Magisters flew overhead in cruciform formation by way of tribute.

As there was still a couple of hours to go before the Pope's arrival at the park, they were entertained by the Garda Band, the No. 1 Army Band, Our Lady's Choral Society, The Chieftains, Bernadette Greevy, Frank Patterson and a choir of 6,000 drawn from parishes throughout Dublin.

When the Pope's helicopter finally arrived in the park it was greeted with a burst of cheering almost drowning out the sound of the chopper. Finally the Mass began at which nine cardinals and one hundred bishops assisted. Considering the massive crowds, at times I found the silence at appropriate moments fascinating, as the multitude hung on the Pope's every word. My team's particular responsibility was for the security of the hosts which were contained in bowls on long lines of tables to the side of the altar area. About 2,000 priests distributed communion to the people in the corrals. Everyone with security responsibilities were particularly vigilant when the Pope descended the steps to board the Pope-mobile. When the ceremonies and speeches concluded, and as the Pope and his entourage were leaving the altar, a large number of us linked arms and formed a protective circle as the crowd began to surge forward. It would be several hours before I exited the park and although it had been a long day I am delighted to have played a small part in what was a momentous occasion and one that anyone who witnessed it will always remember.

Everyone in Ireland at the time will have his or her own particular memories of the occasion and much has been recorded in word and on film for the benefit of future generations. Naturally I made my own record of the event using my eight-millimetre movie camera.

The 1980s heralded the beginning of another half century for St Theresa's Unit and the Unit Council considered a number of ways of marking the period. The idea of involving all sections in a Scout show formed. As a model, we discussed the 'Gang Show' first created for Scouts by Ralph Reader in 1932 and popular across the Irish Sea. From time to time the sections would perform short humorous sketches or dramas for the amusement of their parents. The performances were far from faultless but the mistakes and minor disasters seemed to add to the parents' enjoyment of the evening. The idea was to build on these experiences and develop a show to a much higher standard and acceptable to a public audience.

A committee of volunteers was formed consisting of my wife Bernie as chairperson, Nora O'Brien secretary, Peter Lawlor treasurer and John Lawlor, Paddy Commerford, Alan O'Connor, Kay Lawlor and myself. The first meeting took place at my house and all agreed to engage a professional to produce the show. Freda Bannon owned a stage school in the area, and Bernie and I visited her at her home to discuss the idea. Freda agreed to take on the challenge of turning hikers into dancers but to do this she would have to have access to a piano in the Den. As you can imagine, this would not be a standard piece of equipment in the average Scout hall so an appeal to the Gay Byrne show was made and a listener from Tallaght donated a piano. With the piano installed, rehearsals got under way immediately and continued for sixteen weeks.

Freda worked wonders with the young performers who were quick to learn, arranging great song and dance routines. The leaders were a different matter and most started out with two left feet but with time and practice could 'turn a heel' so to speak. The singing aspect was a different matter and much less of a problem as this was something the Unit was good at. Scouting songs were well practised for many years but there were a lot of unfamiliar ones to be mastered. To help with this I prepared song sheets and also wrote the words on large sheets of paper, which were pinned to the walls of the Den. This was helpful when combining singing with a dance routine.

The show was divided into four main elements or themes including Cockney, Highland, Minstrel and Celtic and each required specific costumes and settings. The parents co-operated 100 per cent by fitting out their sons with general costume items such as white shirt, long black slacks and black trainers and socks. Other less commonly available items such as minstrel and Scottish hats, polka-dot waistcoats, bow ties, kilts and other bits and bobs were provided by Freda, the parents, and leaders. Props were another matter. For the Irish scene I constructed a folding Irish cottage, complete with window and half door; traders' stalls for the cockney scene, and twenty-four claymores or swords for the Scottish scene. I painted hanging items for stage decoration including various emblems and a large backdrop depicting St Paul's Cathedral. To make this, Bernie sewed some bed sheets together and I hung this on the outside wall of my office at the back of my house and sketched and painted the facade on to the sheets, using a ladder to reach the higher areas.

Up to this point, each of the sections rehearsed independently but as the big day drew closer it became obvious that the Den could not accommodate the entire cast for final rehearsals so the first of these took place in Archbishop Byrne's Hall. As St Anthony's Hall in Merchants Quay was to be the venue for the show we managed to hold a couple of rehearsals there, including the final dress rehearsal.

Finally, with great anticipation the cast of seventy-nine assembled back-stage on Tuesday night 20 May 1980 for the first performance and included the following.

Cub Scouts: Pail Byrne, Paul Elliot, James Tracy, Stephen Keogh, Jim McDonnell, Brian Dempsey, Anthony Byrne, Kenneth Waldon, Alan Fitzgerald, William Styles, Justin Moore, Michael McDonnell, Edward Fitzsimons, Mark Freer, Shane Brown, Stephen Staunton, Keith Mackey, Gary Cassidy, Barry Brown, Mark Byrne, Mark Kelly, Gearoid Simms, Christopher Cassidy, Mark Dowling, Keith Boyle, Dermot Tisdale, Mark Reilly, John McEnroe, Dean McEvoy, Archie Raeside junior, Noel Monaghan, Nigel O'Brien, Arthur Boyne, Ciaran Grumley, David Murphy, Desmond Dunfey.

Scouts: Ciaran Long, Kevin Ross, Paul O'Dowd, Kenneth Power, Richard Logue, Colm Comerford, Maurice Peterick, David Murphy, Joachim Nolan, Ian Fitzpatrick, Tony Hayes, Gary Dowling, Robert Moore, Barry Sheridan, Noel Cusack, Martin Raeside, Bernard Dowling, Martin Farrell, Laurence Cassidy, Con Logue, Patrick Gibney, Daniel Tracy, Denis Blake, Ciaran Launders, Stephen Ross, Mark McEnroe, Paul Fitzsimons, Terry Kelly.

Leaders: Brenda Keenan, Gillian Roche, Paddy Comerford, Archie Raeside, Paddy Sullivan, Tommy Hartnett, John Lawlor, Tony Crowley, David Morrissey, Alan O'Connor, Peter Lawlor, Frank Lawlor.

Guest Artists: Ned Bowes, Donal Dixon, Jack Raeside and Eamon Bolton.

Freda's husband Jimmy Ryan took charge of all stage matters including sound and scene changes assisted by Dave Cusack, Declan Lahiff, Rory Dooley, Paul Bramley, Alan Fitzgerald and Gary Spain. Back stage and looking after the costume changes were Madge Murphy, Alice Blake, Betty Cusack, Rita O'Dowd, Nell Morrissey, Bernie Raeside, Kay Lawlor, Carmel Cleary, Patricia Peterick, Marie Murphy and Maurine Tisdall.

With the hall filled to capacity the house lights went down, the audience fell silent and the show began as Freda played the 'track–cart' music on the organ. Marching and singing to the rhythm of the music the Cubs appeared on stage from the wings followed by the Scouts and then the leaders. With the entire cast on stage they gave a lively performance of rousing Scouting songs which the audience clearly enjoyed as they joined in by clapping to the beat. I sounded a bugle call from back stage which signalled the end of the scene and all marched off-stage to enthusiastic applause.

Following the grand opening the compere and comedian Ned Bowes dressed as a Cub Scout, entering stage left, he asked the audience in pantomime style, 'Has anyone seen any Scouts, I'm supposed to meet them here?'. When the audience responded appropriately he introduced the first act, the 'Cockney' scene.

Dressed in polka-dot hats and waistcoats, this song and dance routine was performed by the leaders to the music of 'the Old Kent Road' and 'Maybe it's because I'm a Londoner'. In top hat and tails, Paddy Commerford joined the chorus singing, 'I'm getting married in the morning' followed by 'Get me to the church on time'. As the song was coming to a close he was hoisted on to the dancer's shoulders and carried in a horizontal position off stage. Jack Raeside then performed 'The Streets of London' to his own guitar accompaniment. In my best cockney accent I sang 'Henry the Eighth' and then the entire compliment danced energetically as we sang 'Any Old Iron' bringing the first scene to a close. While the stage was being prepared for the next act Jack returned to front of stage, having changed out of his cockney costume to sing 'The Black Velvet Band' and 'Henry my Son'.

The Scottish scene came next, opening with the Scouts appearing on stage dressed in tartan forage caps and sashes, white shirts and navy trousers and singing 'Marching through the Heather' as they gave an excellent performance of figure marching. All the adults dressed in traditional Scottish costume for this element of the show, which added interest, and a touch of colour to the performances. Paddy Commerford joined the act singing 'Roaming in the Gloaming' and 'I Love a Lassie'. Guest artist Donal Dixon then took centre stage to give a great solo performance.

Brenda, Gillian and Alan formed a trio for a dance routine to Freda's rendition of 'Mac Dougle MacNab and MacCoy' followed by a Scottish sword dance. Playing 'Scotland the Brave' on the bagpipes I came on, joined by the Scouts, figure marching as I played. This concluded the first half.

America was the destination for the opening of the second half and began with the Cubs performing a Minstrel scene. They sang 'Are you from Dixie?', Toot-Toot-Tootsie', 'Carolina in the Morning', 'Yankee Doodle Dandy', She's my Lady Love' and 'Swannie'. Part of the routine was performed on a darkened stage and the special lighting produced a reflective effect on the costumes adding an interesting effect.

Eamon Bolton sang 'Slow Down, You're Going Too Fast' while the stage was being prepared for the next act which we called 'Home Again' featuring Irish scenes. This began with Ned Bowes portraying an old Dubliner, telling a story to children as they sat in the glow of a street lamp. The story was told with great feeling, as Ned recited 'Dublin in the Rare Old Times'. A change of tempo followed as the leaders, dressed as freedom fighters and bearing rifles at the slope, marched on stage singing 'Slatery's Mounted Foot'. The next act included a bit of humour, with Gillian, Brenda and Paddy Sullivan acting out the storey of 'Whistling Phil McHugh' as Frank Lawlor sang the song. The curtain closed on an excellent performance that was well received by the audience judging by the applause. To allow time for the stagehands to remove the Irish set, Jack sang 'Whiskey in the Jar'.

For the finale, the curtains opened to reveal the entire Unit in uniform with a glowing campfire in the foreground. The list of campfire songs included 'Ram Sam Sam', Phil the Fluter's Ball' and 'Moses Saw a Light a Shining', and in traditional Scout gangshow style the final song was 'Crest of a Wave'. With all on stage standing to attention, I played 'Lights Out' on the trumpet signalling the end of the show.

Judging by the standing ovation and rapturous applause, the show was a great success and it was gratifying to know that the effort everyone had put into it was worthwhile. The following night, as I visited the dressing rooms to check that all was in order for the second show I noticed a sense of excitement and an eagerness to repeat the success of the previous night. Everyone gave of their best and sure enough it was a triumph.

At the end of the month the committee met once more at my house and all were in agreement that the project was well worth while, gave the entire unit something to focus on and achieved the objective of creating a sense of unity between all sections.

Word of the show travelled fast and soon requests for a repeat performance were being received. At the Unit camp in Carestown House in June the idea was put to all sections and past members. The general feeling was that it would be almost wasteful of talent and resources not to do so and many expressed a genuine interest in threading the boards once more. It was also suggested that although profit was not part of the original objectives, this time around, perhaps it could be a source of fundraising.

The committee re-convened in the middle of September and again in October to allocate areas of responsibility for staging the show for the second time. At this point I had taken on the role of Unit Leader for a year so I wrote to the parents advising them of the decision and thanking them for their earlier support. I wrote a piece for the newspapers about our show business endeavours and a few of us appeared on Radio Telefís Éireann on the Jimmy Greeley 'Club 80' radio show and Radio Dublin.

This time around, only four rehearsals, including the dress rehearsal were required before the opening night. Two shows took place on 11 and 12 November and again they were both successful. The Chief Scout, Joseph Lawlor was so impressed that he instigated a National Scout Gang Show to be held annually.

Locally, there was a definite surge in interest in Scouting in the following year as applications for membership increased. This was such that the Unit Council decided that a second Cub Pack was needed to satisfy the demand. Eamon Bolton and Frank Lawlor agreed to lead the new group and on Saturday 21 March they held the first meeting. My son Archie was now ten years of age and had a couple of years under his belt as a Cub Scout so to help in the formation he transferred to the new group as a 'Sixer'. A few days earlier the unit took part in the St Patrick's Day Parade along O'Connell Street and my son Martin was part of the colour party. Throughout the year all sections continued to be active in Scouting matters and leaders and parents met regularly to ensure the Unit remained vibrant. The troop travelled to Switzerland in July for annual camp and in August the Unit Camp was held in Larch Hill where a dedication ceremony took place to unveil a memorial plaque to Paddy Downes.

The unit had been meeting for nineteen years at its present location and it was decided to purchase the building. Negotiations were successful and when the contract was signed the property was vested in the 'Scout Foundation', ensuring that for all time it would be used exclusively for Scouting purposes. By the end of the year I had prepared drawings and other necessary documentation and made application to the planning authorities for permission to retain the building as a Scout Hall. This was granted in April 1982 but there were objections from a few residents and it went to appeal. We received a lot of support from many institutions and individuals, including residents, in our reply to the appeal and eventually permission was granted, subject to a few minor conditions. Having established ownership and legal use of the property as a Scout meeting place, it was now felt that the future needs of the unit could be advanced in confidence.

8

AIR SCOUTING

Prior to and during my term as Unit Leader, I was deeply involved in an area of Scouting new to Ireland called 'Air Scouting'. This was a concept that flourished in other countries and I had felt for a long time that it could also be popular here in Ireland. When I discovered others were of like mind I immediately became involved.

In 1979, Mr Pat Lea presented a report on Air Scouting to the Programme Committee of the National Executive Board. This report outlined the concepts of introducing air activities to the Scouting programme. The same year, representing Air Scouts, I attended a seminar in Broc House which was set up to consider future developments in CBSI.

Mr Joe Madden, the first director of this new programme, was appointed in 1980 and the following year Joe gathered a group of leaders around him to form the first Air Activities Advisory Team (NAAT) and we met regularly to discuss tactics. The same year saw the investiture of the first Air Venturer Group at Kilkenny Airport. The group was under the leadership of Mr Pat Meade, Unit Leader of the 6th Kilkenny. At the event, I was pleased to hear the chief Scout Joseph Lawlor say:

> With a membership of 33,000 plus, it is inevitable as Ireland becomes more involved with the age of technology, that many of our young members will be interested in these type of activities, aeronautical subjects included. CBSI is an educational organisation with a unique progressive training programme, and to remain committed to these important aspects of our association, we must maintain our demonstrated ability to change with the times and ensure we provide our young members with interesting activity programmes, suitable to both their interests and age groups.

I arranged to meet the Officer Commanding the Irish Air Corps at Baldonnel Aerodrome and outlined the air activity related objectives of the Scouting movement. The idea was received warmly and I immediately arranged a guided tour of the base for the Scout Troop and from then on good relations with the Air Corps continued. I was aware that the new Venture was going to take up a considerable amount of my spare time so I passed the reins of the Unit Leader position to John Lawlor. It was my strong belief that there was sufficient variety of aeronautical subjects to warrant a dedicated Scout Troop so I proposed to the Unit Council that I be permitted to establish a second troop within the unit to cater for young people who had an interest in aviation. Approval was given on the undertaking that I would not recruit from within the existing troop and I agreed to this with the exception of my two sons Martin and Archie who had for some time been active building and flying model aircraft and were keen to become involved.

To be based or have regular access to an active flying site would be the best possible situation for any group of young people interested in aviation so I wrote to Captain Darby Kennedy at Weston Aerodrome requesting a meeting. We met in October and I outlined ways in which the Air Scout programme might benefit from contact with a private flying club and how the club and aviation in general might gain from developing this interest in young people. The captain appeared to be receptive to the idea and agreed to give it serious consideration. Meanwhile I designed the Air Scout logo and a series of merit badges and wrote a few articles for the *Scout Leader* magazine to promote Air Scouting.

Captain Kennedy offered the use of a building at Weston Aerodrome as a Scout Den. The building was in need of some refurbishment and I was delighted when leaders and friends of the 35th helped with decoration and installing electricity and water and in June 1982 I was in a position to begin recruitment. Paddy Comerford, Martin Raeside and Stephen Carey were my Assistant Air Scout Leaders and Archie Raeside Jnr was the first Air Scout followed by Tom Bannon, Keith Maher, Tony O'Brien, William Raeside and Ian Kelly.

These boys made up the first patrol and called themselves the Vampire Patrol after the Irish Air Corps jet trainer, the De-Haviland Vampire. For Scout Troops who wished to make air activities a regular part of the programme, the NAAT decided that such troops would receive 'Flight' designation, so this new group would be referred to as No. 1 Flight.

Training of the Air Scouts got under way, which included the normal Scout programme activities such as first aid, fire lighting, hiking, camping, canoeing orienteering, and pioneering along with the air-training programme. This involved subjects like flight safety, air traffic control, principals of flight, navigation, metrology and aircraft recognition. The programme also included aeromodelling which involved building chuck gliders, control line and radio-controlled model aircraft.

Being based on an active airfield the boys gained valuable hands-on experience and under supervision became practised in ground handling when aircraft needed to be moved. As experience and confidence grew they got to assist with aircraft refuelling and radio and telephone duties. It was not unusual for the captain to call into the Den and ask for a Scout or two to move an aircraft. He would always approach a leader when requesting help and one day he looked into the Den and not seeing me he said 'Where is your skipper?' From then on the boys referred to me as skipper. Less exciting but every bit as important were the jobs of picking up stones from the runways and washing aircraft. In return for the assistance they were providing, Captain Kennedy took the Air Scouts flying from time to time which made it all worth while.

On 9 June 1983, almost a year after start up, Fr McArdle, the Unit Chaplain of the 35th, invested the new Air Scouts at Weston Aerodrome. Mr Joseph Lawlor (Chief Scout) and Fr Larry Mulligan (National Chaplain) were flown into Weston for the occasion in a club aircraft piloted by Revd Fr T. McCarthy, Chaplain to Aer Lingus. Other special guests present were Colonel Brian McMahon of the

Irish Air Corps and his wife, and Captain Kennedy and his wife. Captain Kennedy was presented with a plaque and his wife a bouquet of flowers to mark the occasion. The director of Air Scouts, Mr Pat Meade, presented the Air Scouts with various merit badges. The icing on the cake so to speak, was when the captain took some of the Air Scouts flying in a Tampico light aircraft.

The articles in the *Scout Leader* magazine on Air Activities for Scouts were beginning to have some effect as more and more enquiries were received. The next unit to take positive steps towards engaging in air activities was Kilmacud. This was spearheaded by Captain Kevin Byrne and within a short time he had enough enthusiastic leaders and Scouts to establish the second Air Scout Troop, No. 2 Flight.

The members of No. 1 Flight now had enough training and hands-on experience of hiking and camping skills to equip them for an extended under-canvas adventure, namely, Annual Camp. Evaluation of sites at Glenmalure, Abbeyshrule and Birr were carried out to decide the most suitable venue. Birr Airfield was selected and Mr Frank Egan the proprietor of Dooley's Hotel was most helpful with the early preparations. The permission to camp form was completed and submitted to National Headquarters and approval of the Director of Camping was duly received.

I investigated the possibilities of the troop flying in light aircraft from Weston to Birr but found it difficult to firm up on pilots who would be available on the day and opted for the conventional route by road. On the evening of Friday 15 July, camping and personal equipment was packed into Jack Raeside's van. By car and van the journey was uneventful except for a stop at Portlaoise to stretch our legs and buy ice-cream and sweets.

Mr Paddy Corboy, the owner of the airfield, gave us the choice of camping on the airfield or in an adjoining recently mowed field. Because cattle grazed freely on the airfield, I opted for the mowed field which offered greater safety and fewer disturbances from roaming cattle. After unloading the tents, boxes of equipment, pioneering wood and personal kit from the van, everyone enthusiastically began the task of setting up camp before nightfall. The Vampire Patrol, under the direction of Patrol Leader Tony O'Brien pitched their tent and dining shelter and decided the layout for their campsite. Using timber posts and sisal, separate areas for dining, sleeping and cooking were staked out. The leaders meanwhile pitched the main store tent nicknamed 'Fenian Street', their sleeping tent, the dining shelter and a tent to house eleven powered model aircraft, fuel, batteries and other essential model aircraft equipment. With the campsite well in hand and the construction of 'altar fires' almost completed, everyone agreed that supper, followed by bed and lights out would round the day off nicely.

The first morning of camp began with reveille at 8 a.m. and a run led by Martin got everyone off to a good start or at least it got the circulation going. After a wash and breakfast, the campsite was completed including dining tables, toilet tent, flagpole and the unfinished altar fires. Meteorology was included as one of the projects and, as a great believer in learning by doing, I had constructed a Stephenson's Screen to help understand the subject. While the rest of the patrol prepared lunch, Keith and William built a stand on which to mount the weather station. After lunch I introduced the subject by explaining the importance to airmen of understanding weather reports and showed how, by the use of the wet and dry bulb temperatures, the relative humidity and the dew point could be obtained. With the weather station set up, the first readings were taken and entered in the weather record sheets. Entries were made daily throughout the camp as often as the programme allowed.

After sitting around for a while, an energy release game always proves popular and this took the form of a frisbee game. Even more popular was flying control line model aircraft. This form of aeromodelling is no longer very popular and perhaps an outline of what it entails would not go amiss. Basically it's an aircraft model flying in a circle attached to control wires which are attached to a handle held by the pilot. With radio control flying restricted by expense, the golden years for this form of powered model flying stretched from the mid-1940s to the early '60s and continued in popularity for another decade or two. I built and flew my first model of this type in the early 1950s and later introduced the hobby to my children. I was confident the Air Scouts would enjoy the experience. A variety of materials and construction methods can be employed to build the model but sheet balsa wood of various thicknesses is the most basic. Various craft skills and safety in the use of basic cutting tool, adhesives and finishes, as well as attention to detail in the construction of a model, are all beneficial attributes acquired by the pupil along the way. For some, starting the engine was a bit daunting but after some practice the technique of flicking the propeller without it smashing into a finger when the engine fired was achieved. To achieve maximum revolutions some fine-tuning was required by adjusting the mixture control or needle valve and the compression screw. It is always rewarding to see a young person develop an interest in a new activity and in this case master the skills to take control and fly a powered model aircraft well.

At 5 p.m. the boys began to prepare and cook their first dinner of the camp which consisted of bacon, cabbage and potatoes followed by stewed apple and custard, tea and biscuits. The training in fire lighting and cooking on the many previous hikes and weekend camps had prepared them sufficiently to allow them get on with the task unsupervised but, as was standard practice at all meal times, the end result was checked by a leader. The standard was fairly good, with some room for improvement, but as the camp progressed they could not be faulted. The cliché 'hunger is good sauce' was indeed relevant. A day in the open air combined with an active programme brought about such enthusiasm in cooking that Stephen Carey (quartermaster) had only to call out 'QM' and almost instantly Keith was by his side to collect the ration for the next meal. I purchased the provisions on a daily basis and these were stored in 'Fenian Street' for distribution by the troop QM. The daily menu was varied, interesting and, above all, nourishing. For the next nine days the programme was as varied as the meals with the exception of certain routine tasks. These included the morning run, drawing water, collecting fire wood, fire lighting, cooking and generally keeping the site tidy.

The least popular routine job was drawing water. The source was a tap at one end of the runway, about 400 meters from the site. The water had to be carried in 5-gallon containers. No one was heard complaining and the task was carried out in true Scouting spirit. I don't believe conservation was uppermost in the minds of the Scouts as they used the water sparingly but rather the need to keep the frequency of 'water runs' to a minimum. Getting to sleep for the first couple of nights on annual camp is generally difficult and perhaps the excitement of the occasion or the changed environment is to blame. In general, a wide game or ER (energy release) game before the tidying up of the site and supper each night helps in getting everyone to sleep.

Most of Sunday was an 'off site' day. After breakfast everyone paraded at the flag pole for 'flag-up' and uniform inspection and then off to church in Birr. After Mass the boys followed the tourist trail and engaged in discovering the town. Lunch in town was a welcome novelty, as it meant no cooking. Birr Castle, which contains the remains of the world-famous telescope, was visited in the afternoon and there was great excitement about the contents of the museum and the gardens. As I was duty officer for the day, it was Martin and Stephen who supervised the tour while my place was on site. As it happened, I spent some of the time 'above' the site, having been invited by a local pilot to go flying with him.

The next morning time was allocated to writing postcards home to parents and siblings and while I was in town collecting the daily provisions I posted these. Martin and Stephen meanwhile gave instruction in kite building, signalling and aircraft marshalling. When I got back from town I gave another briefing in meteorology, at the end of which I felt the clouds of mystery surrounding the subject was beginning to lift.

Mr Jack Ryan, the local Scout Leader paid a visit to welcome us to the area and to check that his Venturers had delivered firewood as arranged, which they had not. Without further ado, he headed for the hills and returned a few hours later with a trailer full of timber which he and a couple of helpers chain-sawed into logs. The firewood we had been foraging in the area of the site was by now exhausted and we were glad to get a fresh supply, even though it was somewhat wet. Flying the kites that had been built earlier, then flag down, a wide game, and finally bed rounded off the day.

Between flag up and lunch on Tuesday, the three hours were spent flying model aircraft as well as a radio-controlled model Archie Jnr had been building prior to camp. It was a high wing monoplane of built-up construction with a 1cc. engine and controlled by a single servo which operated the rudder. As this was to be its maiden flight, everyone was keen to see how it performed. It climbed beautifully to about 100 meters, levelled out and flew the circuit and after about twenty minutes made a perfect landing just in front of the campsite. Further very successful flights were made during the camp but some did require the inevitable retrieves from the tops of trees, fortunately without any damage.

CBSI, at this time, was promoting many new activities in the Scouting programme. Just like air activities, a department was set up to look at ways of encouraging young people interested in marine matters. Some Leaders and Scouts were seeking more and the term 'Sea Scout' was sought after by some members. This was by no means a new idea, and as I mentioned previously in the early years of St Theresa's Unit a Sea Scout section, the 9th Port existed. Mr Paul Dennehy was appointed National Commissioner for Water Activities, charged with the task of bringing this exciting activity to life again. I mention this because the local Scout Troop offered us the use of canoes, which they owned.

From a number of canoes available we selected a one-man and a two-man and carried these to the river near the outskirts of town. With life jackets on and following some instruction in safety procedures, Martin and I took it in turn in the two-man to instruct. A few had previous experience but we decided for safety reasons that a single one-man canoe was enough to supervise as we paddled our way up-river. Going under the Town Bridge gave ample opportunity for practice in manoeuvring. Continuing the theme of water activities, we spent an hour in the nearby swimming pool. Although there were a good number of people in the pool, the style of Tom Bannon whom we regarded as our champion swimmer was noted by the pool supervisory staff. Tom practised daily and was a regular competitor in swimming galas. Two of the troop had missed out on what had been an active and exciting day. Stephen was back on site as duty officer and young Archie was isolated to the leader's quarters with suspected measles.

Arriving back on camp in the evening we found Archie Jnr fast asleep. When he woke up and heard about the great day on and in the water, he perked up and all signs of illness disappeared; it had evidently been a false alarm. The only other medical attention required during the camp was for treatment of horse-fly bites, which nobody escaped. William seemed to be their tastiest dish, with a preference for his left arm. There was also, towards the end of camp, some minor stomach upsets and exhaustion, which eight hours or so of excused duties and a sleep remedied.

As part of the normal procedure for annual camp, it is usual for a local inspecting officer to visit the site and make a report to National Headquarters. This frequently happens without prior arrangement and this was how Jim Kirwan, the Regional Commissioner for Training, appeared on site. Just after dinner and during a period of relaxation I noticed a car drive across the airfield heading for our campsite and anticipated that it was the inspecting officer. I passed the word on for everyone to scramble, and while I engaged Jim in conversation, everything was made ship-shape. So impressed with the campsite and the programme activities he asked that we seriously consider attending his regional camp.

The final project of the evening was designing and building chuck gliders. Everything, from orthodox airplane to tri-plane and delta shape was produced. This was an activity that everyone enjoyed, and no encouragement from the leaders was needed. Even as the cutting blades become blunt, the enthusiasm of the designers was not deterred. By all appearances, new designs would have continued to come off the production line into the early hours of the morning but a final halt had to be called to all this creativity at 11 p.m.

Awakening to another fine day, the usual rise, run, wash and breakfast was quickly taken care of and then the instruction to get into uniform was issued. The programme had indicated that a tour was planned and the leaders were asked if this was on the cards. As leaders sometimes do, the question received non-commital answers such as, 'Maybe,' 'Could do,' 'Might, but maybe not' and so on. Louis could stand it no more and asked how leaders had the ability to plan an activity without releasing all of the facts. However, before the end of camp, he and the rest of the troop were to appreciate the element of fun, which sometimes accompanied surprise. A rucksack containing wet-weather gear and some food rations which included cheese, butter, bread, soup, sliced meat, tea, milk and sugar was placed in the boot of my car. I drove across the airfield and the Scouts were told to meet me at the main gate where each of them were blindfolded and directed into the car. As we drove along, many theories of what was happening were guessed at with nobody getting close. After a twenty-minute drive I stopped the car in Kinnety Village and told them to remove the blindfolds. 'Does anyone know where we are?' I asked and one or two thought they recognised the place but this turned out to be false. I then gave the Patrol Leader Tony a compass and map of the area and then said to the group, 'You are survivors of an air crash, which resulted in temporary blindness and have regained your sight at this location. At a position marked with an "X" on the map you will get shelter, food and medical help, your mission is to find the location and return to this village not later than 17.00hrs.' Before driving off I gave Tony £3 to be used in case of emergency, or spent on sweets if the mission was successful. The challenge seemed less difficult with the prospect of goodies at the end.

The place they were to find was a log cabin situated in the Slieve Bloom Mountains surrounded by forest and owned by the Birr Scouts. The cabin, of stone and timber is of very solid construction, insulated and well suited for winter activities. It is generally booked up for the main part of the summer by visiting troops and groups so the local Scouts use it mainly in the wintertime.

The Vampire Patrol quickly established where they were by simply asking the local people and so, using map and compass they moved off in the correct direction. At one point they asked a man for directions but were unsure about what they were being told and ignored his advice and relied on their own orienteering skills. After a couple of hours, and getting lost only once, the cabin was reached. A group of Venture Scouts were staying at the cabin for a week and welcomed the Air Scouts, sharing a meal together. The Venturers then showed the visitors through the dormitories, the kitchen, toilets and other rooms. The main assembly area featured a large central stone chimney and fireplace with an open hearth. Small stuffed animals such as squirrels were placed in climbing stance on boughs extending from floor to ceiling and looked very realistic and almost seemed as if they might at any moment jump down from their perch. The most dominant exhibit was a fox, which stood in a central position on a large timber mantle.

Having enjoyed the hike to the cabin and the company of the Venture Scouts all that remained was to reach Kinnety Village on time. In the village the £3 was quickly spent but not entirely on sweets (£3 went a long way in 1983) as the shop had a pool table and other amusements at the rear. Finally, all that remained was for me to ferry the patrol back to the airfield where, as they prepared dinner, the highlights of the day were discussed.

The plan was for Thursday to be an on-site day starting with a full kit inspection followed by washing of clothes and some base-oriented subjects. The first part of the programme was adhered to but as the weather was so good no one objected to the alternative of going to the swimming pool after lunch. Walking to and from the pool as well as the swimming activity helped to develop an appetite and an eagerness to prepare dinner, which consisted of chicken, carrots and potatoes followed by yoghurt, milk and biscuits.

Joe Collins, the chief flying instructor, had mentioned to me the probability of being able to take the boys flying at some point during the week but I kept this information to myself so as not to build up false expectations. Joe arrived as the boys were clearing up after dinner so I called them together and told them the planned activities were cancelled in favour of flying. The clean up was taken care of in record time and excitement rose as the aircraft taxied from the hangar on to the runway. The first to go were Ian, who sat in the co-pilots seat and Louis who had not flown before, taking the rear seat. As Louis was being strapped into 'Rallye EI-BFV' he asked, with some concern in his voice 'Where's the parachute?' to the amusement of those with some previous flying experience. Twenty minutes later, on returning from his first flying experience in a light aircraft, his expression had changed to one of excited pleasure. Flying was not a new experience for Patrol Leader Tony and his assistant Keith and I could see that as they disembarked from their latest experience they tried to suppress their excitement in front of the younger members but their expressions revealed just how much they had enjoyed it. An additional passenger made up the third flight with Stephen up front and Archie Jr and William in the rear. For the last flight of the evening Tom took the front seat while Martin took up the rear and did a bit of aerial photography. After an interesting cross-country flight, the trip ended with some passes over the campsite to try for some pictures in the fast fading light. With half flaps set, engine at 1,200rpm and airspeed at 65knots Bravo Foxtrot Victor purred in on finals, setting smoothly on the runway bringing what had been a great day of flying to an end.

While munching biscuits and with a mug of cocoa in hand we sat at the dining shelter and held a sort of debriefing. Having been to Birr Castle and Gardens earlier in the week, surprise was expressed at how small it all looked from the air. On approaching the Shannon, the sun was setting low over the mountains, casting long shadows on the ground, a view seen only from the air which some likened to an oil painting or picture postcard. Joe thought that the young fliers would appreciate other than straight and level flying and so he put the aircraft into the occasional tight turn making the flight a little more exciting. At the end of the outward leg of each flight he asked the way home and to our surprise no one got it right, emphasising how easy it was to become disorientated in the air. Even after lights out and the boys, snug in their sleeping bags, could be heard discussing the day's events.

It was Friday morning and the end of what had been an active and enjoyable week under canvas at Birr Airfield and now the troop assembled at the main gate awaiting the arrival of a minibus to take them to Galway and Salthill. The banker had released all of the remaining spending money and in addition a subsidy was provided to buy lunch. As duty officer for the day, I was confined to the campsite but was fully briefed on the events of the day later in the evening. I busied myself building a woodpile, making repairs to model aircraft and filling water containers and logged thirty minutes flying time in EI–BFV for my pilot's log book.

As the minibus headed west, the Scouts sang songs such as 'Three Blind Jellyfish' and 'There Once was a Wheelbarrow'. The driver sat impassively and endured all, no doubt anxious to reach his destination as soon as possible and dispatch his energetic and happy passengers. Passing through open green countryside for most of the journey, the group expressed surprise at how busy Galway was. Being city lads, they were of course delighted with the variety of shops and keenly set about buying records, teddy bears and other souvenir-type presents for their families. With the shopping spree completed, the minibus then took them to Salthill. Here the sound of arcade games and other amusements was music to their ears as they ran into the maze of amusements to spend the last of their money.

Having had an exciting day, there appeared to be no energy left for singing on the journey back to camp. Back at the site the boys sat (or should I say slumped) around the dining table and when I asked 'Who's for an ER game?' the answer was almost instant and unanimous, 'Not tonight Skip, please'. Then I asked 'Who wants to go to a disco?' and suddenly they all had a new lease of life and were prepared to go instantly but I insisted they prepared and ate a salad dinner first. After the meal, they enthusiastically polished shoes, washed, combed hair and generally made a great effort to look their best.

I had heard about the disco from a member of the Shannon sub-aqua rescue service who organised the event in order to raise some funds. He also offered us the use of canoes, rubber dinghies and other equipment and I acknowledged the offer but had to decline because of lack of time in our programme. When we arrived at Shannon Side, where the open-air disco was taking place, the moon was full and shone brightly, casting its reflection on the still waters of the River Shannon. A huge bonfire blazed nearby, sparks rising from the dancing flames and, to complete the picture, coloured lights flashed on and off to the rhythm of the music.

Even with this great atmosphere, the dance floor was empty so the Air Scouts took the lead, dancing energetically, until the floor was alive with perhaps 200 people dancing and singing. At 1 a.m., I decided it was time to get back to camp, otherwise the boys would be too tired for the next day's events. As they were enjoying themselves, it was obvious they would have stayed longer but in good spirit they accepted the decision and said how much they had enjoyed the entire day.

The decision to delay reveille until 9 a.m. because of the busy day previously was welcomed by leaders and Scouts alike. Tom Bannon was scheduled to compete in a swimming gala and his parents and sisters called to the site to collect him. With weather records being kept daily, a visit to the meteorological station at Birr was arranged. They got an in-depth guided tour of how a weather station operated, and at the end the Scouts produced their own records. The Meteorological Officer compared these figures with the official records and was surprised when they compared very well, which was great encouragement for the Air Scouts to maintain an interest in the subject.

Heading back to camp in late afternoon, Archie Jnr, Ian, William and Keith wanted to stop off in town to do some last-minute shopping and, as Stephen volunteered to supervise the shopping crew, this was agreed. As the shoppers carrying their purchases began their walk to the airfield, the heavens opened and the rain came down in torrents. Attempts to shelter under trees were useless so they continued on. The rain was so heavy that I decided to go and meet them. Five very wet but grateful young men climbed into the car and immediately changed out of their wet clothes when we got back. The heavy rain continued as dinner was being prepared and the boys found it impossible to keep their fire going so they resorted to cooking on gas under the dining shelter. The leaders stuck it out and actually completed cooking dinner on the altar fire although the sausages were boiled rather than fried, because the rain was so intense and every time the lid was lifted to turn the frying sausages the pan filled with water.

At 8 p.m. the choice between staying under the dining shelter and engaging in some activity or having free time and rest was offered. The boys opted for resting and retired to the tent and were happy to listen to the thunder and watch the tent glow in the lightning flashes. A couple of hours later, hot cocoa was prepared for everyone but when

1 The first recruits to No.1 Flight. From left to right, front row: W. Raeside, K. Maher, T. O'Brien, I. Kelly, T. Bannon, A.W. Raeside. Back row: The author, S. Carey, M. Raeside.

2 No.1 Flight on tour of Dublin Airport. Junkers JU52 in background.

3 Tony and Archie Jnr learning to start a model aircraft engine.

4 Initial set of Air Scout badges designed by the author.

5 The first Investiture. Fom left to right, front row: M. Raeside, A.W. Raeside, T. Bannon, W. Raeside, S. Carey. Back row: John Lawlor, author, Ian Kelly, Tony O'Brien, Keith Maher, Joe Lawlor, Pat Meade.

6 Basingstoke Air Scouts visit Baldonnel.

7 The author prior to take-off at Weston.

8 The author, making his way back to earth.

9 The author, strapping in to fly.

Opposite from top

10 Author and his son Archie meeting Douglas Corrigan.

11 Air Venture group, No. 1 Flight.

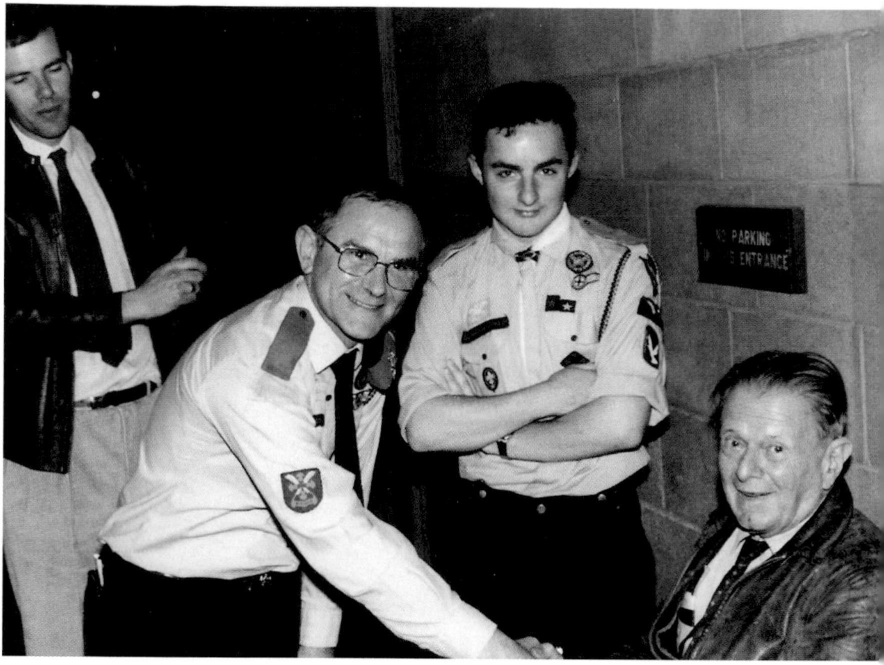
NO PARKING
ENTRANCE

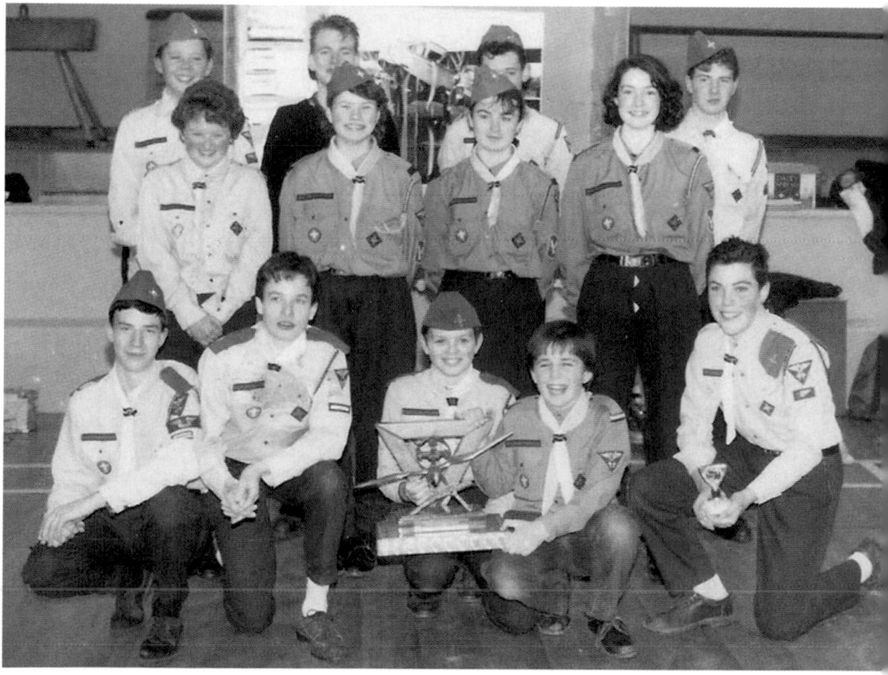

12 The National Air Scout Trophy.

Martin called out, 'Come and get it,' there was no reply for the very good reason that all were sound asleep.

Sunday morning and the last day of camp dawned with everyone well rested for the task of breaking camp, which lay ahead. After the usual start to the day it was in to uniform and off to the local church for Mass. Back at the site most of the personal gear was packed, not forgetting the gifts which were collected from the store tent. Tents were taken down and after cleaning the tent pegs and folding the guy ropes everything was packed in valises. After dinner the rest of the campsite was dismantled and equipment grouped, ready for loading into the van. At arm length, everyone formed a line across the site and moved slowly across the field a few times to ensure every piece of paper, string, wood and anything that should not be there was picked up. With the site looking as if we had never been there we enjoyed some tea and sandwiches and discussed the events of the past ten days, while awaiting the arrival of Jack's van. Some wished it could go on, at least for another few days while others looked forward to getting home to family and familiar surroundings but said they would come back after a few days at home if that were possible. What everyone did agree was that every minute of this the first annual camp of No. 1 Flight was enjoyable, action packed and not to be forgotten.

I sent thank you letters to all that had supported us in the preparation, planning and running of the camp and these were acknowledged by all concerned. In particular Paddy Corboy thanked us for leaving his place as we found it and welcomed us at any time in the future.

Lieutenant Colonel John O'Brien invited me to attend a meeting in the Officer's Mess in connection with the forthcoming Fitzmaurice Air Rally at Baldonnel Aerodrome. This is a competitive event designed to test the flying skill of private pilots. Included is a cross-country element which requires accurate pre-flight planning and navigation and five of the more senior Air Scouts manned check points along the route. Their job was to record each aircraft as it arrived overhead. For the Spot Landing event, lines were painted across the runway a set distance apart and parallel to each other. The rest of the Air Scouts took up a position, one at the end of each line and recorded which line the landing wheels came closest to.

The troop also participated in the Society of Amateur Aircraft Constructors 'fly-in' at Weston, Air Spectacular '83 at Fairyhouse and at the Cub weekend in Glencree where they gave a demonstration of control line flying. At the close of the year, Martin, Tony, Keith and Tom decided to go on a midnight hike on Christmas Eve. Off-road or cross-country hiking has always been the preferred option and as this hike across the Dublin Mountains progressed, snow began to fall. The hikers enjoyed the seasonal atmosphere for the first few hours but as the snow fell heavier and visibility became reduced, Martin decided it was becoming unsafe to remain in the mountains. He led the group to the youth hostel at Glencree where the caretaker let him use his telephone to contact me. It was midnight when I received the call and Martin explained that the roads to the hostel were impassable and that he would take the group out of the valley and meet me up on the main mountain road.

With screen wipers going full speed to keep the snow from building up on the glass and using dipped headlights to reduce the blinding reflection I peered ahead until eventually I came across the group. Back at my house they climbed into sleeping bags and made themselves comfortable on the living room floor for what was left of the night. It was a busy Christmas morning in our kitchen as the family and young hungry hikers prepared breakfast. With everyone fed and watered so to speak, we then attended the Unit's traditional Christmas Morning Church Parade at 8.30 a.m. at which Martin sounded the salute at the consecration. He had taken on the role of bugler from me a year or so previously and I was happy to pass on this function at the many Unit and Regional events.

9

GROWING INTEREST

The attraction of Air Scouting continued to take hold as the Kilmacud Scout Troop established a dedicated Air Activities section as No. 2 Flight. Captain Kevin Byrne, a pilot with Aer Lingus and Scout Leader with the unit was the founder. In June 1984, a year after setting up, they held their investiture at the aviation museum at Collinstown, which we attended.

Membership of No. 1 Flight continued to grow and as Tony O'Brien, Keith Marr and Andrew Egan passed the Scout age of fifteen years we established an 'Air Venture' section. The Vampire Patrol now consisted of Patrol Leader Ian Kelly, Assistant Patrol Leader William Raeside and Air Scouts George O'Brien, Carl Hammond, Robert Casey and Nicholas McCann. A second patrol called the 'Marchetti' consisted of Patrol Leader Tom Bannon, Assistant Patrol Leaders Archie W. Raeside and Air Scouts Robert Rafter, Marcus Lynam, Brien Costello, Aaron Smith, Martin Egan and Pierce Warfield. The boys decided the name for their patrol, choosing another of the Irish Air Corps aircraft, the 'Marchetti Warrior'. The Patrol Leaders and Assistant Patrol Leaders attended a weekend training course at Larch Hill early in the year to help them in leading their patrols.

At local and national public events, Scouts were regularly called on to sell programmes or assist in stewarding and this, for many units, was a means of earning some much-needed funds. At Air Shows, Air Scouts who had sufficient training were called on to assist with aircraft handling and marshalling. On safety grounds it was approved by National Council to introduce a uniform variation that pilots and Scout Leaders would recognise at a distance and so avoid the possibility of a non-air Scout being in close contact with 'live' aircraft. For Air Scouts, a blue forage-type hat would replace the Scout beret and blue epaulettes would be worn. To source the new hats at a reasonable cost was proving difficult until my cousin Carmel McKeown who was an excellent seamstress came to the rescue and produced the initial batch for our first investiture. As numbers grew and demand increased, the Scout Shop found a manufacturer who could provide a continuous supply.

There were many visitors to our Den at Weston from Scouting and Aviation circles who were interested in seeing what we were about. One such visitor was Captain Arthur Wignall who was at that time the Irish Aerobatics Champion and a former European Champion. Whenever he flew into Weston, the leaders were happy to suspend whatever activity was being engaged in at the time to allow the boys to converse with him. He patiently listened to their many questions and explained the answers in great detail. I recall the boys asking him prior to take off, to do a four-point roll as he flew out of Weston and he, as always, obliged. His enthusiasm for flying touched the boys, as did his death. On the first Sunday in April 1984 he was killed during an aerobatic display in his Pitts Special on a beach at Strandhill, County Sligo. After a career with the RAF he had come to Ireland in the early 1950s to fly with Iona Airways. For seventeen years he flew under contract for Aer Lingus in the Middle East and Africa. At the time of his death a friend wrote in appreciation:

> The tragic death of Arthur Wignal has deprived the aviation community of one of its most colourful characters. Well known for his incredible antics in his Harp Lager Pitts Special, his place and name at all Irish aviation shows and demonstrations was welcomed by all, may he rest in peace.

As mentioned previously, Captain Kennedy regularly called to the Den requesting the help of Scouts for some task on the airfield or in the office. On one such occasion he noticed two rabbits hanging on the coat hook on the back of the door. 'What's with the rabbits?' he says. I explained that one of our projects for the day was to teach the Scouts how to skin and cook a rabbit. He then said, 'Well done, every boy should know how to skin and cook a rabbit.'

Although Weston Aerodrome was the centre of activity for the Air Scout section of the 35th, strong links were maintained with the unit by way of general local and regional events and of course the Unit Council and Leaders meetings. In fact, this year the Air Scouts took second place at the regional Scout Quiz, won five medals at the regional cross-country race, and three gold and two bronze medals at the Scout swimming gala. Martin Raeside and his uncle, Peter Blosse played trumpets at the Regional Mass. At the National Beaver Day the Air Scouts put on a display of model aircraft flying lasting five hours.

It was decided to further extend the Den at Arbutus Avenue. I designed and obtained planning permission for a 100 per cent expansion and my brother Jack was contracted to build it. In the early stages, I helped with the building of a boundary wall. With the wall at about 2.5 meters, high I walked off the end of the scaffold one day. I attribute this to the fact that I had recently acquired new spectacles which happened to be bifocals and not being used to them, misjudged the end of the planks. I was fortunate to fall on to a pile of sand, but my left hand made contact with some concrete blocks, which was used to contain the sand. There were lacerations to the palm and the pain indicated that there might be some damage, so I went to the hospital. An x-ray confirmed that two middle fingers were broken. The affected fingers were folded against the palm and the hand cast in plaster. Although it was a little awkward changing gear and the likes, the club fist did not prevent me from returning to the site and, in my spare time, I painted notice boards for Larch Hill and wrote articles for the *Scout Leader* magazine.

At this time, someone had given my name to Fr M. Connolly, a priest at City Quay church. He wanted me to do some artwork and other small jobs for him. Having seen my hand in plaster, he called to my house one evening with a glass-fronted, six-centimetre-diameter, circular locket containing a number of relics which had been part of the ceremonies at a recent Seaman's Mission. He suggested I make the sign of the cross with the locket over the injured hand each day for a week, which I did. When, after three weeks I returned to the hospital to have the plaster removed, the nurse warned me that because the fingers had been bound in a clenched position for so long, it would be difficult to straighten them and would have to return for physiotherapy. She also said that on removing the plaster there would be an odour from damaged skin. When the dressings were removed the skin abrasions had disappeared, there was no smell and when she said 'try to straighten your fingers' I did so with no difficulty whatsoever. She consulted with a doctor who ordered an x-ray. On seeing the result, the doctor seemed surprised that there was no sign of any damage. Naturally I was delighted to have no further hospital visits or after effects.

For annual camp 1984 we decided on Abbeyshrule Airfield. My contact for securing the venue was Sammy Bruton, formerly of the Irish Air Corps and then owner of Bruton Aircraft Engineering based at Abbeyshrule. Maurice Cronin, one of the best known personalities in Irish aviation, also warmly welcomed us. In 1965, he became the first Irish private pilot to achieve an instrument rating on his licence and five years later he was the first Irishman in history to hold a balloon pilot's licence. Maurice worked with Sammy and his home was adjacent the airfield which he gave me a key to for our use if and when required.

On 5 August, the thirteen Air Scouts taking part in the camp were transported to the site in three cars driven by Martin, Stephen and myself while Jack brought the camping equipment in his van. The usual priority was to pitch the sleeping tents and the marquee followed by building altar fires and tables and finally setting up boundaries. With the campsite set up to everyone's satisfaction the programme swung into action. The main attraction for this year's camp would be the Abbeyshrule 14th Annual Fly-in and Air Show. In between the programmed activities, the Air Scouts were called on to assist in moving aircraft, a job they were by now well practised in.

Taking advantage of local amenities, we engaged in some rod and line fishing in the River Inny which flowed into Lough Ree. Another enjoyable water activity was boating on the River Shannon. Naturally the highlight of the camp was the Air Show at which those Air Scouts who were sufficiently skilled directed arriving aircraft to their designated stand using marshalling bats. This was an extremely responsible job and I could not but be proud of their achievement, especially when pilots approached me and commented on their clear signalling.

The show was officially opened by radio presenter Derek Davis and began with a veteran and vintage car parade. Aerial displays included the Dunlop Pitts Special, the Irish Air Corps, model aircraft, balloon ascent, micro lights and aerobatics by Paul Van Lonkhuyzen in a Robin and by Sammy Bruton in his Stampe. The Fornier Duo performed a brilliant aerial ballet in gliders.

The show also featured an autogyro display, parachuting and a static display of many vintage aircraft and included a First World War Fokker DV11. It had been a thrilling, exhilarating and very successful air show and as the Air Scouts took a well-earned rest that evening they were all happy to have had some part in it.

The second week began with another air-related activity. As we had learnt the previous year how easy it was to become disoriented when flying, tutoring in aerial navigation had been on going since then. It was decided to put what had been studied to the test in a practical way. The troop was divided into groups, or flights, of three and each flight had to prepare a flight plan involving a triangular cross-country course. Paddy Moran, piloting a Robin, agreed to fly the course, as directed by the young navigators on board, and every flight succeeded in directing the aircraft back to the airfield. Paddy remarked on how impressed he was at the navigational skill of the Air Scouts. For those who had not already achieved it, the Navigator Merit Badge was awarded.

In addition to the aeronautical aspect to the camp, there was the usual camp routine: sports activities, swimming, church parade and shopping day. On the final day of the two weeks, survival shelters were constructed by the boys from natural woodland materials in a dense forest a few miles from the airfield. That night they enjoyed the delights of a teenage disco in the Rustic Inn. After the disco there was mixed feeling about spending the night in the survival shelters, but the challenge was accepted in true Scouting spirit and next morning all claimed to have had a good night's sleep. Sleeping rough in a forest was a new experience for everyone and, judging by the general comments, there was an appreciation of their normal warm room and comfortable bed. Back at the airfield, after a wash and a good breakfast, the campsite was dismantled and by mid-afternoon we were on our way home.

Shortly after this camp Tony O'Brien, one of our founder members, and at this stage a junior leader, was accepted as an apprentice aircraft technician with the Irish Air Corps.

Mike Hobbs, leader of a well-established Air Scout Unit based in Basingstoke in England, arranged a camping holiday in Ireland for some of his members. Through CBSI Headquarters he made contact with our unit and we were happy to act as hosts. We agreed to provide the necessary tents and camping equipment so on breaking camp at Abbeyshrule I headed straight for Larch Hill to pitch the marquee for their use. This was the first contact with Air Scouts from outside of Ireland. Over the next two days, Mike and I discussed many topics in relation to Air Scouting, which was to prove useful into the future. He had travelled to Ireland in his Land Rover and brought some parachutes, hoping to do some parascending but was having difficulty securing a suitable site. I arranged, through the Irish Air Corps for this to take place at Baldonnel Aerodrome the following Saturday. Mike and some of his group were qualified to instruct in the sport and this gave some of us an opportunity to experience the thrill of parascending, which became a new interest for me which I would actively pursue.

Year three (1985) for No. 1 Flight began with a visit to Dublin Airport, to view the Aer Lingus Boeing 747. John

Malloy, father of one of our Air Scouts arranged for the group to go onboard the aircraft. Although the boys were familiar with how an aircraft flies, they openly expressed amazement at how such a massive structure with an all-up take off weight of 300 tons and with more than 400 passengers could take to the air. As they looked out through the windows of the six-metre wide passenger cabin, one of them was heard to say 'You could land a Piper Cub on one of those wings'. This was of course an exaggeration but an indication of how impressive the sixty-metre wingspan was.

Perhaps it was at this point that my son Archie developed a desire to one day fly a 'Jumbo'; a dream fulfilled twenty-three years later. In the meantime, he began his flying training under the instruction of Captain Kennedy in exchange for working at Weston during the school summer holidays.

The assistance given by the Air Scouts on Saturdays was proving very useful and the captain requested that a couple of Air Scouts be available on Sundays. Naturally this was on a voluntary basis and applied to the more senior Scouts and a roster of enthusiastic helpers was drawn up.

On the subject of being helpful, for any Scout Troop the support from parents should not be underestimated. We were fortunate to have this and when parents meetings were called, the mothers always provided more cakes than could be consumed. The fathers also answered the call and were not slow in helping out when there was a bit of plumbing or electrical work to be taken care of or to provide transport when required.

Aaron Smith's father Richard came on board as a leader. Richard had experience as a Sea Scout in his younger days and perhaps it was this that prompted him to donate a rowing boat. The reasoning behind the idea of the boat was that, as the River Liffey ran alongside the airfield, it could be used for rescue in the event of an aircraft 'ditching' in the river. Repairs to the hull were required before the boat could be painted and launched and the boys, under Richard's supervision carried these out. After four months' work the craft was ready for the 'blessing of the boats' at Ringsend on 15 June. With air activities being the main interest, enthusiasm for sailing was limited but a few of the boys did enjoy this added interest. By coincidence, a small flying boat visited Weston, thus combining the two interests. The pilot offered to take two Air Scouts on a flight experience and Martin Egan and Aaron Smith were the lucky passengers. The flight took them south-west to Shannon. They later described the new experience of landing on water along the River Shannon and how the aircraft taxied up a slip-way at the pilot's home. His mother treated them to chips, ice-cream and lemonade before they returned to the river to take off for the return flight to Weston.

Although the membership had increased, there was only six available for summer camp. Because of the low numbers I decided that this was an opportunity to visit as many airfields as possible during the two weeks and, to this end, Pierce Warfield's parents provided us with a Renault Traffic van. On 7 August, the tour of Irish airfields began by heading for Birr in County Offaly. As the tents were being pitched, two aircraft from Weston arrived overhead and executed manoeuvres, making it clear that they were aware of our presence. The camp coincided with the International Scout Jamboree which was taking place at Portumna in County Galway, so we included a visit to this spectacular event. Portumna will be remembered for many things, not least the wet weather, which prevailed throughout the duration of the camp and was referred to as 'Port Mud'. For the first time, air activities were included as a base at the jamboree and this was organised by the Air Scouts from Kilmacud. On the night of the closing ceremony, 10,000 Scouts from all over the world assembled in one area holding lighted candles as they all sang the 'My Little Light' song, a real sign of international unity, peace and hope. A large balloon with a trailing line of the flags, representing all of the participating countries, ascended into the night air as exploding fireworks lit up the night sky while the huge crowd cheered.

The next day we set up camp at Abbeyshrule airfield which was planned to coincide with the annual air show. Having helped out at the air display the previous year the club once again called on the air Scouts to engage in some aircraft marshalling before and after the show. Johny Malloy had flown down from Weston in his Piper Cub and we all got to fly with him. During the three days at Abbeyshrule we also revisited the local swimming pool.

The next airfield to camp at was in Limerick. Once again we received a warm welcome from the Limerick Flying Club and Paddy Power provided flying experiences in 'Rallye EI-BDK'. At Shannon Airport the group enjoyed a detailed guided tour of the control tower conducted by the various departments based there. This gave a good insight into the many important aspects of air traffic control which involve the movement of every aircraft that enters or leaves Irish air space as they are picked up by radar and displayed on the computer screens.

Nuala O'Donoghue of the Hibernian Flying Club arranged for us to camp at Cork Airport for Air Spectacular '85. The weather continued to remain inclement and even as we pitched the tents on the wet grass we began hearing from officials that the show, which was to take place the next day, was in doubt.

From early morning fog hung over the airport and everyone hoped that it would clear, but unfortunately this was not to be and the decision to cancel the show was announced. The cancellation was unfortunate but the next day there was a lot of flying activity to witness as visiting aircraft took off for their home bases and this helped to stem the disappointment. Almost directly over our campsite, the Irish Air Corps put on a spectacular helicopter display, which lifted the spirits of the Air Scouts.

A stopover at Kilkenny completed the two-week familiarisation tour of Irish airfields. Although bad weather prevailed throughout the fortnight, everyone enjoyed the somewhat unusual nature of this mobile annual camp and many old acquaintances were renewed and new friends made.

My usual involvement with the Unit Council and the Building Committee continued throughout the year. With the new Den nearing completion, I took on the job of cladding the fireplace with stone. A very successful weekend combining Scouts and Air Scouts was held in Slane and we travelled together in my brother Bill's coach. The

Air Scouts attended a special display of the *Zenith* aircraft given by its test pilot, followed by an evening lecture about the aircraft in Bolton Street College. They also demonstrated control line model aircraft flying for five hours at the National Cub Day event. Another busy time involved assisting at the Society of Amateur Aircraft Constructors fly-in.

With the downturn in construction activity continuing throughout the 1980s, I spent much of 1986 travelling to and from England to undertake architectural stone design work for an Irish-based company. Having met Mike Hobbs and a few of his senior Air Scouts the previous year when they came to visit Ireland, I decided to accept his invitation to attend some of his troop's regular meetings at Basingstoke. Other contacts visited included the 7th Teddington Air Scout Group, Jim Davidson at the Scout Resource Centre at Gilwell Park and Baden-Powell House. I found these visits useful in forming programme ideas for our own Air Scout meetings and activities.

I had been flying solo in light aircraft for three years and decided to achieve a similar standard in the sport of paracending. After making enquiries I discovered a club operated at North Weald airfield just north of London. The opportunity seemed too good to miss so I joined Harley Chutes and travelled on average twice a week for training. Within three months I had achieved my objective of flying solo using square canopies.

David Cahill and Andrew Masterson, both of them pilots, came on board as leaders and were more than welcome as the flight continued to attract new members. They generally flew in to Weston from Iona Flying Club for the weekly meetings and on many occasions took Air Scouts flying which proved very popular. They were of great benefit in many ways becoming enthusiastically involved in the Scouting ethos and gave great encouragement to all.

The combination of increasing membership and some of the founder Air Scouts becoming of Venture age required that we book a group on to a Patrol Leaders' training course which took place at Aughavana.

I believe it safe to say that every Scout remembers the day of his or her investiture and with this in mind it is important for Scout leaders to plan the event carefully so as to make it a special occasion. Last year No. 1 Flight held their investiture at Casement Aerodrome Baldonnel at the invitation of Lieutenant Colonel John O'Brien. Taking place in a hangar with Air Corps Beech King aircraft as the backdrop gave an appropriate atmosphere to the occasion. There is a sense of achievement for the Scout and pride for the parents as each in turn marches up to the flag to recite the 'Scout promise' and have the troop neckerchief placed around his or her neck. After the ceremonies there was a reception in the apprentice school for all, followed by a tour of the base conducted by Lieutenant Colonel O'Brien. A demonstration of model aircraft flying by Martin Raeside concluded the day's events.

This year, the investiture took place at Weston and the large attendance of parents, leaders of all sections of the unit, and invited guests were accommodated in the main clubroom. Most of the Air Scouts were interested in model making and to encourage this hobby a Model Engineer Competition was introduced and the entries were displayed for all to see. Prior to the investiture ceremony, a film was shown of the previous year's annual camp. An occasion such as this, with family and friends present, was also a good time to award achievement badges.

Merit badges have always been a way of rewarding Scouts for achieving certain standards in a subject and for traditional Scouting there was available a great variety of subjects to choose from. Not so for air activities, so I designed a series of badges to cover air-related subjects such as air spotter, air mechanic, airman, meteorology, model making, navigation and paracending. As knowledge increased, the Air Scout could progress to skills award badges such as Air Scout, Senior Air Scout and Master Air Scout. Wings awards included aircrew or half wing brevet, parachute wings and pilot wings. At this investiture, eight of the more senior Air Scouts achieved the air crew badge. To achieve this badge, a Scout must first have completed the Master Air Scout requirements and have ten hours' flying experience in a number of alternative ways. There is also a written test of eight questions to the standard of the private pilot's licence. The practical element involved a walkabout of a light aircraft in the presence of a qualified pilot and covering safety/document/engine/airframe and flight planning. It is also necessary to demonstrate a practical knowledge of navigation and be capable of lecturing Scouts on aviation topics.

An International Air Scout Jamboree was taking place at Wroughton Airfield near Swindon and I was confident No. 1 Flight would enjoy the experience of sharing some time in the company of like-minded young people in England. Knowledge of this camp came to light earlier in the year while visiting Jim Davidson at Gilwell Park and I asked that we be included in the event. In June, I received approval to camp overseas and the required international letter of introduction and other documentation. Preparations got underway and the necessary paperwork including menu, programme, and travel costs were submitted to National Headquarters.

The response was good and involved three patrols consisting of sixteen Scouts and a well-attended parents' meeting was held to outline the nature of the camp and give each the opportunity of raising any concerns they might have. Richard Smith and his wife Kay assisted me in the running of the camp. The original route involved a number of train connections and long waits on railway platforms so I looked at alternatives. I discovered that Slatterey's Travel Agency in Tralee operated a coach service from Rosslare to London. They agreed to make a small detour from their normal route and let us disembark close to our destination at Swindon. It was the day before departure but the dash to the B & I booking office was worthwhile to put the new travel arrangements in place. A couple of telephone calls to Mike Hobbs in England and he agreed to have us collected from the bus at Swindon.

At 8 a.m. on Saturday 19 July, some very excited Air Scouts gathered at the gates of Weston Aerodrome to await the arrival of the minibus from Celbridge Transport, which was to take us to Rosslare. With haversacks stowed away, a group photograph was taken by one of the parents, Mrs Jones-Ladbrook, which appeared in the *Leinster Leader*. There were five more Scouts to collect at Rathfarnham and with these on board we were finally on our way. Near

Enniscorthy I became somewhat apprehensive about reaching the boat on time but kept these fears to myself so as not to cause any concern. The plan was to board Slatterey's coach at the port and drive on to the ship but when we arrived there was no sign of the coach. At the B & I office I was told that the coach had gone on to the ship and we had less than five minutes to get aboard. It would take much longer than this to unpack the minibus and walk the distance, so the B & I official issued a handwritten pass for our bus to bring us aboard. As we were stowing our luggage the *Innisfallen* set sail; it could be said that it was a close call. The Scouts, of course, were unperturbed and every corner of the ship was investigated and the ship's food sampled.

On docking at 4.10 p.m., we quickly cleared customs and, with a certain amount of difficulty, the Slatterey's driver packed our gear into the luggage compartment. About an hour from Swindon there was a scheduled stop for passengers to have something to eat. Finally, thirteen hours after leaving Dublin we were met by Mike Hobbs and Terry Bridge and transported to Wroughton Airfield in two Land Rovers and a Transit van. On arrival at the airfield we saw that the Basingstoke Air Scouts had begun to erect our tents, so we immediately changed into camping clothes and got stuck in. Tentage for our host troop and us included twenty-one tents, six dining shelters, a store tent and a marquee. Tables, seating, basins, Billy Cans, and gas was also provided for each patrol and the leaders. With the campsite complete, a game of football followed and finally a light supper of drinking chocolate and biscuits was welcomed by all. The strict rule of silence after

11 p.m. was easily observed, as 500 tired air Scouts bedded down for the night.

The following is a synopsis of the week-long camp and the activities undertaken. Events were arranged by allocating tickets each evening for the activities that were to take place the next day. Included was glider, hot-air balloon, kitemaking, nature trail, flight briefing, chariot race, obstacle course, a radio course, orienteering, abseiling, canoeing and use of life jackets. With the young participants having a keen interest in aviation it is not surprising that the really popular events were flying experiences in such aircraft as the D.H. Chipmunk, Hercules C130 and gliders.

Paragliding was also included. As mentioned earlier, this was a sport that the Basingtoke Air Scout group were involved in and a number of their leaders held instructor ratings. The sport had not yet been established in Ireland by any organisation, and even in the UK only a limited number of Scout groups had it as part of their programme of air activities. For the young Scouts who were taken aloft by an instructor, the experience was clearly a great thrill. Separate to the scheduled programme for the camp two members of the Defence Forces requested that they avail of the launch facilities to evaluate the flying abilities of an experimental canopy known as a 'Bird Wing'. On completion of their evaluation they asked if any qualified paragliding pilots would like to fly it solo. I was surprised that there were no takers so I volunteered to give it a try. Before take-off I enquired if there was anything in particular I should watch out for and was assured that it was much the same as other canopies I had flown. The launch was good and I released the line at perhaps 2,000 feet. Making 360- and 180-degree turns were a joy to perform and after twenty minutes and many circuits of the airfield I decided to descend. At 300 feet altitude on final approach I realised there was no penetration into wind and the rate of decent was hardly noticeable. A feeling of helplessness came over me as the parachute seemed to hover. I then became aware that the distance to the landing area was increasing; the canopy was flying backwards.

As I continued to float backwards, I considered making a turn to the left or right but, having lost another 100 feet or so, I quickly discarded the idea. I felt I was now too low to make a recovery if some cells collapsed in the cross wind. Pulling down hard on both toggles I tried to stall the canopy. This was something I had done successfully while in training over the past couple of years, but on this occasion nothing happened. I tried this manoeuvre once more to no avail. I then considered pulling down on the front risers but dismissed this idea knowing that excessive downward pressure on the leading edge could collapse the canopy completely with possible disastrous consequences. Discovering that I could safely make slight left and right changes to the flight path, I decided that the best course of action was to hold on to what control I had even if I was flying backwards.

The very slow decent allowed me turn my head to observe what lay behind me in the distance. The perimeter of the airfield was fast approaching and I estimated that the landing was very likely to be beyond this and not into the hedgerow each side of the public road. There was a wide space between two small forests and I decided to steer a line in that direction. The distance between me and the launch area had increased to the point that I could no longer recognise the faces of the group standing their. I remember thinking, 'you are on your own'. As I crossed the perimeter road at a height of fifty feet I could see that some people had come to realise my situation and a small group rushed to the Land Rover and drove rapidly in my direction.

Confident of my ability to execute landing rolls in various directions I now gave serious thought to performing a good backwards landing roll, something I never thought I would ever have to perform. The ground seemed to rush past at tremendous speed as my feet brushed the tips of the wheat stalks. When knee-high into the wheat, I flared the canopy and made a good backwards landing roll. After standing up I collapsed the parachute, gathered it up and made my way to the road where a group of relieved colleagues helped me over the fence and back to the airfield. Somebody remarked 'every landing you walk away from is a good one'. Although it was a successful flight, it was an exhilarating experience to say the least and in hindsight perhaps not one of my better decisions.

Camping standards were maintained and time was found for the usual site and kit inspections. Cooking was arranged by patrol, with an inspection for flair and quality at the main meal each evening. There was also time to visit town as well as the RAF Museum at Middle Wallop and attend an air show at Yoerelton. Sir Bernard Chacksfield, Air Vice-Marshall of the RAF presented the prizes at the closing ceremony. When presenting the best individual prize for aircraft recognition, he expressed surprise that it was won by an Irish Air Scout Pearse Warfield with Aaran Smith a close second. The Air Scouts from the 35th Dublin also took first prize for best team on camp. Many friends were made by Air Scouts and leaders but the best measure of the success of this camp was the desire on the part of most who took part for it to go on longer.

The weather for Air Spectacular '86 at Baldonnel was very good, unlike the disappointment of the show in Cork the previous year. It was by now routine for Air Scouts to assist in areas such as the aircraft-parking zone, the static display area and traffic control. Two new flights had been established: No. 3 from the 49th Dublin (Swords) founded by Mr Michael Rogan and No. 4 Flight, St Colman's (Newry) by Mr John McCourt. With increased members, we were able to give additional help by providing stewards in the VIP and spectator areas and help with the sale of the *Flying in Ireland* magazine. The show was a great success and of course every individual spectator will have his or her own particular highlight to remember.

For me it involved the *Iolar*. This is the name, which means eagle, given to the first Aer Lingus aircraft, a DH Dragon. On 27 May 1936, the company operated its first flight between Baldonnel and Bristol. The original *Iolar* was sold to Olley Air Services a couple of years later and on a flight from the Scilly Isles to Land's End in 1941 is said to have been shot down. The existing *Iolar* is a sister ship of the original. It was built in 1936 and test flown by the great Geoffrey de Havilland on 18 April of that year. It had a number of owners up to the time: it was bought by Mr J. Cleary of Mullingar and brought to Ireland in March 1950. Captain Darby Kennedy became the new owner five months later and it was used for light charter work and pleasure flying out of Weston for the next nine years.

My particular interest in the aircraft relates to my Uncle Paddy. What I recall of the story, which I heard when I was very young, was that Paddy was terminally ill with cancer and the family were keen for him to travel to the shrine at Lourdes. All pilgrimages at that time were undertaken by sea and overland but my uncle was too ill to endure the journey. His brother, Andy, formulated a plan to make the trip by air. His enquiries revealed that to receive approval for the flight it was necessary for a qualified doctor and certified nurse to accompany the patient. With these requirements met, he then arranged with Captain Kennedy to make the flight in the DH Dragon.

Captain Kennedy eventually sold the aircraft to Aer Lingus and flew it to Dublin Airport, painted in the original *Iolar* colours in September 1967. Passengers travelling through Dublin Airport will remember the *Iolar* on display in the departure hall for many years. As the fiftieth anniversary of Aer Lingus approached, John Malloy, quality insurance inspector in the airline's Maintenance and Engineering Department and the father of one of our Air Scouts who I have referred to previously, proposed that the aircraft could be made airworthy again as part of the celebrations. Supported by Captain J.J. Sullivan, a pilot with Aer Lingus, the proposal was accepted and work commenced. The airframe was generally in good condition and only a small number of wing ribs needed repair or replacement. Metal areas were x-rayed and control cables examined and anything requiring treatment or replacement was attended to. The plywood floor and side wall panels were replaced by Brendan O'Donoghue of the Irish Air Corps. At one point John gave me a small piece of the original floor as a keepsake.

John replaced the original covering with a polyester-based fibre and other work was carried out by members of the airlines Maintenance and Engineering Department. The *Iolar* returned to the air on the fiftieth anniversary of its maiden flight in April 1986 and here it was four months later at Baldonnel. An RTÉ crew was about to be taken on a flight to do a feature on the famous aircraft and John asked if I would like to be included in the flight – what do you think was my response? No marks for the correct answer. An official ticket was promptly issued – which I still have – and after being interviewed by the TV crew, relating the story of my uncle, we all boarded the *Iolar* and took off for what was a memorable and most enjoyable flight around the area.

To mark the fiftieth anniversary of the *Iolar*'s first Baldonnel to Bristol flight, celebrations were held in the Officers' Mess at which Bernie, some Air Scouts and I attended. A re-enactment of the flight was planned, but due to 75-kt winds this was postponed to some weeks later.

The Fitzmaurice Air Rally took place the following month at Weston and again the *Iolar* was one of the principal attractions. As well as performing in the air, it remained at the aerodrome for the day on static display. Air Scouts assisted with the ground handling and directing the general public to view it. All the Air Scouts camped out that weekend which left the Scout base free for flight briefing and administration. The boys also took on a catering role and prepared and served tea and sandwiches for the participants.

Still on the subject of the first Aer Lingus flight, Kevin Byrne, with the help of Captain Donal Foley Operations Manager, arranged an exchange between Air Cadets from the Bristol area and Irish Air Scouts. Sean Dolmen, John Volves and Dave Roberts of the Air Cadets travelled via the Aer Lingus commuter service and a tour of the facilities at Dublin Airport was conducted for them by the Kilmacud Air Scout group. The exchange involved Irish Air Scouts Kevin De Hora, Eoin Farren and Aaron Smith who were taken on a day-long tour of the Bristol Filton Aerodrome facilities. These include aircraft manufacture and testing, engine testing, and flying training and there was a variety of aircraft types to be seen. To complete what could be termed the 'Year of the *Iolar*', Air Scouts were part of a large audience which attended a lecture about the *Iolar* presented by the Royal Aeronautical Society on 8 December at Trinity College.

For the second year running, some of the Basingstoke Air Scouts came to Ireland and joined with Weston Air Scouts in hiking, bowling and air-related activities at Weston and Dublin Airport. On 25 September 1986, celebrations were held at National Headquarters to mark the CBSI Jubilee year at which I was appointed National Co-ordinator for Air Activities.

10

A NEW ROLE

Although I had resigned as leader of No. 1 Flight at the end of 1986 to concentrate on my new role at national level, I continued to visit Weston throughout 1987 to do some private flying. Together with the National Officers, I attended monthly meetings at Larch Hill and National Headquarters which were essential in reviewing all aspects of the workings of the association.

To formulate a programme of air activities to suit all ages, I assembled a group of interested leaders. This was known as the Air Scout Advisory Team. We met at Headquarters for the first time on 3 February. These meetings proved very useful in compiling a Progress Scheme Information Pack, outlining how to combine Air Activities with the normal Scout programme for individual Scouts and dedicated patrols or troops. A pocket-size book was also published which set out the requirements of each of the Air Activities Merit Badges, skills awards and other challenges and included a section to record the date each award was achieved.

In an effort to promote an awareness of the sport of parascending, I made contact with the Wild Geese Parascending Club in Newry and over three weekends many enjoyed the experience. As well as being a new venture for a lot of people, it was run on a sponsorship basis in aid of the Irish Wheelchair Association and the money paid for a holiday for forty wheelchair users.

I introduced a National Air Scout Trophy in the form of a large brass eagle mounted on a mahogany base and a series of competitive events was formulated and competed for by as many as seven teams over a weekend in April at Larch Hill the following year.

At the Society of Amateur Aircraft Constructors (SAAC) 'fly-in' at Weston in June 1988, the 35th Dublin Air Scouts exhibited a full size one-man glider. This was donated by Mrs Mary Byrne in kit-form and had been owned by her late husband who unfortunately never got to build it. Under the direction of Richard Smith, and with a lot of help from members of the SAAC, the aircraft was completed, minus the fabric covering and received an award at the event.

To assist air-minded Scouts in acquiring information on aviation matters, I set up a library. Some material came from personal donors and more I purchased from the aviation bookshop. The list of material available was given to all established groups and published in the *Scout Leader* magazine.

That year a number of Air Scouts and I got to meet a famous aviator. It was during a tea-break in the late 1950s that I first heard the name Douglas Corrigan. I was a young airman, recently graduated from the Technical Training Squadron with the Irish Air Corps and honoured to be a part of a small group of aviation professionals. These were the staff of the Aeronautical Engineering section at Air Corps Headquarters. With 'wad' (cake) in one hand and a cup of tea in the other I would listen respectfully to my peers as they recounted exciting aviation exploits. The story of 'Wrong Way Corrigan' fascinated me and I immediately placed him in my hero's list. Little did I know that twenty years later I was to meet this remarkable man in person. It happened when he came to Ireland as guest of the Royal Aeronautical Society, Dublin Branch and Aer Lingus.

At Trinity College, on 19 July 1988, he appeared as guest of honour to celebrate the fifteith anniversary of his historic flight. It would be safe to say that everyone in the hall knew the story but here was the man himself, wearing the original leather flying jacket taking the rostrum to tell his story in person. On 18 July 1938, he landed at Baldonnel Aerodrome in a Curtis Robin aeroplane, having flown the Atlantic from Floyd Bennet Field in America. He was alone and was airborne for twenty-eight hours. This was not the first time the Atlantic had been flown but it was the first time 'by mistake'. He was twenty-six years of age when he bought the single-engine Curtis Robin. As an aircraft mechanic, he not only serviced the aircraft himself but also rebuilt it in the five years preceding his great adventure. Money was scarce in the 1930s but his dedication to flying helped him through many lean and hungry times.

The aircraft was given an experimental aircraft certificate (restricted licence) for a 6,000 mile round trip from California to the east coast and back and Douglas Corrigan was told that if he got to New York in one hop, a full licence would be considered. On 9 July 1938 he did get to New York, flying non-stop for twenty-seven hours and landed with four gallons of fuel left. The next day he flew the short trip to Floyd Bennet Field and filled the big tanks with 320 gallons of fuel, intending to leave at midnight. He had difficulty explaining the clearance he had been given in California but eventually he was cleared to take off at daybreak on Sunday 17 July, lumbering into the air after an exceptionally long take off run, he set a westerly course. Or did he?

The compass he used was a type which had parallel lines on a top ring which had to be oriented for heading and an arrowhead showed the correct end of the lines. To fly on the selected heading, the aircraft turned until the compass needle was parallel with the lines on the top ring. The arrowhead, however, was at the wrong end of the lines, which went unnoticed by Douglas Corrigan, and so instead of travelling westward he was on an easterly course. Weather conditions were bad and as he flew on in fog, cloud, and rain he made only the occasional glance at the compass to see that the needle and lines were parallel.

On Monday 18 he descended to 3,500 feet and noticed sea under him. It was at this point that he realised that the arrow on the compass was at the wrong end; this meant he was over the Atlantic and not the Pacific. With only three hours of fuel left, it was a relief to see land in the distance. Passing over Donegal, he continued towards the east and once again approached a coastline. The relatively short distance from coast to coast convinced him that he was over Ireland. Turning south over Belfast he followed the coast and finally made that historic landing at Baldonnel. Wrong way or not, it was a tremendous achievement in a single-engine light aircraft. It was due in no small measure to the skill and determination of its brave and remarkable pilot. He was an overnight celebrity and was received by the President Douglas Hyde and members of the government.

After his presentation at Trinity College, this eighty-one-year-old aviator made himself available to all who wanted to meet him. It was indeed a great pleasure for me to have met Douglas 'Wrong Way' Corrigan in person and I am pleased to have a photograph of my son Archie and myself meeting the great man.

In the Phoenix Park, the Model Aircraft Council of Ireland put on a spectacular model aircraft display as part of the millennium celebrations and Air Scouts and Venturers from Dundrum assisted by keeping take-off and landing areas free of spectators.

In the aviation calendar, Air Spectacular at Baldonnel was once again the highlight event and all of the Air Scout sections as well as the Basingstoke Air Scout group put in a very busy and responsible day amidst live aircraft. The weather was less than ideal with 50kt winds and rain the order of the day but nevertheless, as usual, the show was a great success.

A meeting to evaluate the Air Scout Progress Scheme was held on Sunday 27 November in the Swords Scout Den. The Units taking part were Weston, Kilmacud, Swords, Newry, East Finglas, 10th Sligo, 1st Tramore and

8th Waterford. In all, sixty-four Patrol Leaders, Assistant Patrol Leaders, Venturers and Leaders took part, and everyone actively contributed. All aspects of the programme were discussed and there was no shortage of ideas from the young air-minded Scouts. An aircraft recognition slideshow took place and to round off the day there was the opportunity to take the controls of a radio-controlled model hovercraft with varying degrees of success.

John Condon from RTÉ arrived at Weston with a film crew on 17 December to make a documentary about air activities for Scouts. The final edited version of the day's filming was broadcast on the RTÉ 1 *Joe Maxi* programme on 12 January 1989. The film begins with a young Air Scout receiving instruction on how to fly a control line model aircraft followed by a radio-controlled model hovercraft being flown along the runway. In the next scene, a patrol is shown how to carry out a pre-flight walk around on a Minerva aircraft. Traditional Scouting is included as a Scout sends a message using semaphore flags. Subtitles appear throughout the film, and in this case, explain that the signal spells out J-O-E-M-A-X-I. Model aircraft construction comes next, and then David Cahill explains the subject of navigation to a patrol. It was at this time that the membership of CBSI began to include girls and this is reflected in the documentary, as my daughter Berni gives a class in First Aid. The final scene shows Air Scout Mathew Bates walking boarding a Cessna aircraft followed by in-flight film of Mathew receiving hands-on flight training from David Cahill the pilot.

Appearing on national television gave Air Scouting a great boost and as a result I received letters from Scouts from all over the country. Membership increased considerably this year due to the publicity.

An aeronautical craft and aircraft recognition competition was held in the Phibsboro Scout Den in February. There were four categories in the craft competition: aviation project, static scale, diorama and flying model. There were forty-three entries and the winners were No. 1 Flight and Nos 3 and 4 Flights as runners-up. In the aircraft recognition competition for Scouts, first, second and third were Swords, Newry and Swords. In the Venture section the order was Weston, Kilmacud and Weston.

In the same week the film on Air Scouting was broadcast, I wrote a number of letters of sympathy in relation to the Lockerbie Air Disaster. These included the American and British Ambassadors to Ireland, the General Manager of British Midlands in Derby and Pan Am in Shannon as well as the Chief Commissioner of the Scout Association Lockerbie district for their services to the community in the aftermath of the disaster. I received acknowledgement letters from all. Many readers will recall the horror of Pan Am Flight 103 exploding over Lockerbie in Scotland, killing all 259 people onboard as well as eleven on the ground. The aircraft involved was a Boeing 747, which took off from Heathrow at 6.25 p.m. on 21 December 1988; about thirty minutes later it exploded. The nightmare for the residents of Lockerbie was just beginning. In backyards, on fences and on rooftops as well as surrounding fields covering an area of fifty square miles, pieces of bodies and wreckage landed. Burning fuel from the aircraft as well as the damage from the impact completely destroyed twenty-one houses. In the Air Scout page of the *Scout*

Leader magazine the details of the disaster were printed. It referred to Dumfriesshire Area Scouts carrying out rescue work both as Scouts and in other capacities. The person first involved was George Stobbs, both Police Inspector and Assistant Area Commissioner for Scouts in the county. He described the scene as being, 'as close to hell as I ever want to be'. As reports came in that debris was scattered over a wide area, Venture Scouts were called out. Many of them were also members of the local Mountain Rescue Team. Mr Stobbs contacted the Area Scout Commissioner, Marilyn Park, to inquire if Lockerbie Scouters were safe. She reported that one Scout suffered the loss of his mother, father and sister when the plane crashed in the middle of Lockerbie. The Scout hall at Lockerbie was opened up as an emergency centre for children, while their parents helped at the scene of the disaster. Scouting was in the front line of rescue work, providing a messenger and 'Go-for' service in the major operations centre in the Lockerbie Academy. Scouts provided a link for various emergency and community services and carried messages to the American Ambassador. They distributed emergency information leaflets and provided support to the local community. The effects of what was subsequently proven to be a bombing was to be felt worldwide as the flight held passengers from twenty-one countries; but particularly in America as 189 of the people onboard were Americans and it would be eleven years before investigations came to a conclusion.

Involvement with the unit continued by way of monthly meetings with the Unit Council, the sixtieth anniversary Mass in February and a special anniversary weekend at Larch Hill in July where, with others, I received a plaque for service and made a life member. No. 1 Flight held their investiture on 21 October this year in the 35th Den. As usual, proud parents were present and this year this included Bernie and I as our daughter Bernadette and some of her friends were invested as Air Venturers in No. 1 Flight. This was special as they were the first females to join the group.

Having been appointed a director with the National Executive Board (NEB), it was a particularly busy year which included the regular board meetings as well as a leaders conference, working committee meetings, commissioners conference and the National Council and of course the NAAT meetings.

On the aviation front, the Scouts and Venture Scouts spent a weekend in June at Clonbulogue airfield and over the three days everyone got to leave the ground. Attendance at Air Spectacular and the SAAC fly-in had by now become an annual event and again the organisers appreciated the support of Air Scouts.

I managed to fit in half a dozen lessons in 'glider' flying this year. I also introduced Bernadette to the sport and her instructor remarked that she was a natural. It was a special year for my son Archie as he received the President's Award from the President of Ireland, Patrick Hillary at the Royal Hospital.

I was anxious to organise another paragliding event but hoped to hold the event closer to home this time. There was a problem with arranging insurance south of the border for CBSI members to paraglide, which is one of the reasons why we held the previous outing in the north. Enquiries indicated that this matter could be resolved so I contacted Mike Hobbs in Basingstoke and he kindly agreed to provide the necessary equipment and qualified instructors to make it happen. Late on Friday evening on 18 August, I got a telephone call to collect the insurance cover note from Headquarters which I did. Later that night I collected a marquee in Mike's Land Rover and finally arrived at Clonbulogue airfield after midnight. Unfortunately, the letter setting out the terms of the insurance cover had a signed handwritten note at the bottom that cover only applied if the cover carried by the Basingstoke group also applied to CBSI members. This of course was not the case, which is why I requested cover for our members. The following day it was embarrassing to have to tell the large group assembled that they could not fly. Although there was disappointment all round, the news was accepted gracefully and all took part enthusiastically in the ground training which Mike and his team provided. They also enjoyed watching the paragliding skills of the Basingstoke group.

The venue for the National Air Scout Trophy Competition was Casement Aerodrome, Baldonnel by arrangement with the Irish Air Corps. The Scout and Venture teams decended on the camp on 3 December 1989 on a cold but bright and dry morning for what was to be an action-packed and enjoyable day of air-oriented events. Having assembled in the gymnasium the competing teams lined up on three sides of the basketball court and listened attentively as I outlined the day's programme. Kevin Byrne then paraded over fifty excited competitors to the Helicopter Squadron hangar where Sergeants Dick Lynch and Dick Sullivan presented a very interesting and informative lecture on the role of the Alouette three and Dauphin helicopters.

Leaving the hangar, the group then re-assembled on the tarmac to witness a real life rescue exercise. Captain Sean Murphy flew the helicopter while Airman Kieran Tobin was the winch operator. The squadron members had prepared a quiz around the content of everything the Scouts had witnessed and this was implemented later in the day.

The next base in the competition was aircraft recognition, presented by Richard Smith and David Cahill.

Following lunch in the new dining centre, the teams rotated through a number of bases including aircraft parts and controls, aviation quiz, helicopter quiz, Scouting knowledge, model making, and aircraft simulator. All of the subjects were approached and presented expertly and imbued the participants with enthusiasm. All of the teams had built dioramas depicting helicopters and P. Waldron and P. Keenahan judged these air-sea rescue scenes. Mr Keenahan also ran a base on the variety of aircraft modelling possible. The final results showed all events to be closely contested and the event was clearly enjoyed by all that took part.

The second edition of the Air Activities Progress Scheme book was published in 1990. Preparation of the draft layout, with special consideration of the suggestions from all levels of the membership, and proofreading consumed a considerable amount of my time the previous year. Colm Kavanagh, a member of the editorial board of the *Scout Leader* magazine organised the printing. The convenient pocket-sized book allows for recording personal details.

It also contains a form, or 'authority to fly', that must be signed by parent or guardian before a leader can allow their child or ward to fly as a passenger or under instruction in service or civilian aircraft. Principally, the book contains the requirements of each of the Air Activity Merit Badges, Skills Award Badges and other challenges all the way to Pilot and Parachute Wings. The launch took place in the Mews at the rear of National Headquarters on 10 April and those in attendance included National Officers, National Commissioners, Scouters, Venturers, Scouts and special guests from civil aviation organisations and clubs.

Powered model aircraft hung from the walls and ceiling and a colourful display of posters and photographs set the atmosphere as I opened the proceedings by outlining the objectives of the scheme and the progress made since 1982. Mr Michael Hassett, the Chief Commissioner, then performed the official launch on behalf of the Chief Scout Paul Ring. In his address, he commented that I had been enterprising in overcoming many obstacles and had in developing the Air Activities Progress Scheme brought together a core of people committed to making air activities a developing, existing and adventurous thing but principally an achievable attraction. After thanking him for his encouraging comments, I announced the availability of another new book called *Skysport Guide* edited by Madeline O'Rourke who was one of the guests in attendance. I mentioned the book as it is about sport and career opportunities in aviation and would be of particular interest to school leavers and Venturer Groups.

A number of Venturer Groups experienced parachuting through sponsorship for worthwhile charities this year. Kiernan Gildea, the National Commissioner for Scouts completed a seven-day parachuting course in Kent and achieved Scout parachute wings. This surely inspired Scouts to consider air activities. In the preceding year, David Cahill, Andrew Masters, Andrew Vernon and Pearce Warfield from No. 1 Flight and Alan Flynn from No. 3 Flight began careers as professional pilots. Darina Nolan, Venture Leader with the 35th, gained her private pilot's Licence.

The Society of Amateur Aircraft Constructors 'Fly-in' at Clonbullogue was as popular as ever and all Air Scouts and Air Venturers who were there left the ground, some on their first flight experience. The highlight of the year was once again the Air Spectacular. The show, which was being held in Shannon, required a lot more planning. Kevin Byrne, together with a dedicated team, arranged everything and, in the words of Paul Chamberlain the Show Director, every Scout, Venturer and Leader excelled themselves above and beyond the call of duty.

Venturers from No. 1 and No. 3 Flights had an exciting away camp as guests of the Basingstoke Air Scout group. Flying in microlights and parascending training was only a part of the holiday.

Patricia Doyle, National Commissioner for Beavers was keen to have something other than the standard medal as recognition of achievement at the National Beaver Day event. I agreed to give the idea some thought. A figurine of a Beaver came to mind and I set about carving a five-centimetre three-dimensional image. When I was satisfied with the sculpture I made a mould and cast the figure in resin. Finally, I mounted the gold-coloured Beaver on a polished white marble base. Patricia liked the sample so I reproduced this in quantity and some larger variations with the Beaver mounted on a decorative column and including inscribed brass plates.

This interest in carving and casting began when I decided to make a wall plaque of a Rallye, the aircraft I learned to fly in. The hobby continued for some time and I produced plaques of a number of aircraft types, a parachutist and a variety of sculptured trophies for Scouting events and personalised pieces for recognition of service.

Sinead Smith and Grace Rogan of No. 1 Flight took part in Explorer Belt in 1991. This event is run every year by the Venturer Advisory Team and is part of the personal development programme. The highlands of Scotland were the venue, and Grace and Sinead travelled with sixty Venturers making up nineteen teams. The activity involves hiking in pairs over vast distances and meeting and interacting with people in the local communities. They spoke of the beautiful countryside they passed through and good will of the Scottish people and of making lots of friends as they journeyed around Scotland.

The *Scout Leader* has been a great source of information for the membership nationally and, for me, very useful in passing on the message of the variety of air-related activities available. Occasionally interesting articles appeared about Air Scouts in other countries. One in particular comes to mind. It concerns Flying Scouts in Australia and the fact that, in that country where distances are immense and air transport is often the only viable means of travel, Scout Air activities attract a great deal of interest. There is familiarisation flying days for all sections of the movement and for members of the Girl Guide Association. During 1988, the Air Activities Base in Camden in New South Wales had flights for some 4,500 Scouts. In the state of Victoria, where there are two Air Activity Centres, over 1,600 Scouts and Girl Guides experienced flying in light aircraft and twenty-three Scouts trained for their pilots licences. Ten trainees received their licences that year and two obtained Flying Instructor rating. The air centres also include parascending, parasailing, hang-gliding and parachuting.

Back home, two new groups were formed in 1991. These were No. 7 Flight, drawn from the 16th Kildare-Kilcock and started by Nicholas Reilly, and No. 8 Flight from the 91st Dublin with Stuart Garland at the helm. The year began with the Scout Model Aeronauts attending practical workshops in the construction of powered model aircraft. This included methods of construction, airframe types and the finishing and balancing of completed models. The workshops concluded in April with engine care, starting and safety. Flying instruction followed and continued up to the end of May. Baldonnel was the venue for the Model Aeronautics Council of Ireland Nation Competition and the help provided by Air Scouts was appreciated by the MACI. A request to hold a seminar on Air Activities by St Patrick's Region Venturers was taken up in March. The Air Scout Advisory Team as well as guest speakers covered such topics as gliding, parachuting and parascending as well as power flying and aeromodeling.

As 1992 was the tenth anniversary of the foundation of Air Scouting in Ireland, I designed a special badge to mark the occasion, as well as a badge called the 'Aeronautics

Badge' which all Scouts and Venturers could achieve after meeting requirements as set out in the Progress Scheme book. Mary Fricker succeeded in obtaining a sponsor, Goodbody Stockbrookers, to supply a special Air Scout flag so I immediately produced a design approved by the team.

In February, the National AirScout Trophy Competition was again held at Casement Aerodrome with eleven teams involved in thirteen activity workshops. The format was similar to previous years and as usual the co-operation and help provided by Air Corps personnel assured a successful event.

As a member of the Roger Casement Branch of the Organisation of National Ex-servicemen and Women, I was involved in the Unveiling and Dedication Ceremony of the Air Corps Memorial at Casement Aerodrome on 19 July. Air Scouts from the 35th Dublin were also there and assisted by taking on the job of distributing and selling a souvenir booklet specially prepared for the occasion. I subsequently received a letter of appreciation from the chairman for the help provided and also for the donation towards the Memorial Fund from the NAAT. The President of Ireland, Mary Robinson and Patron of ONE unveiled and dedicated the memorial to deceased service personnel of the Air Corps.

A week earlier, Colm McCabe, a fifteen-year-old Air Scout from No. 1 Flight died in an aircraft accident. He joined the Air Scouts at Weston in 1990 and his enthusiasm for flying and all aspects of aviation were apparent from the start. Previously, in 1987, Tony Murphy, an enthusiastic Air Scout Leader with No. 1 Flight lost his life in an aircraft accident. They are always in my thoughts.

Over 200 guests attended a ceremony hosted by No. 8 Flight Inchicore, on the 5 September, to celebrate ten years of Air Scouting. Guests included the Chief Scout, Chief Commissioner, National Commissioners and representatives of the Irish Air Corps and many aviation societies and organisations. In traditional ceremonial order, the first National Air Scout Flag was blessed. I presented appreciation awards to many who had supported and given practical assistance in helping to make Air Activities for Scouts a reality.

With Mary Fricker as my editor, I produced a book detailing the history of Air Scouting in Ireland over the past ten years and this was launched as part of the celebration day. Joseph Lawlor, the Chief Scout, presented me with the CBSI Silver Medal of Merit. Having prepared the programme for the event, this was not something I was aware of and it came as a welcome surprise and something I appreciated very much.

On 22 November, the Aviation Society of Ireland held the first Aviation Enthusiasts' Fair in Wynn's Hotel. It attracted hundreds of visitors and many visited the Air Scout stand and expressed a great deal of positive interest and support for what Scouting was doing by way of helping young people to be aware of aviation as a career opportunity and as a sport.

The second decade for Air Scouting in Ireland began with No. 8 Flight holding their first Air Scout Investiture Ceremony in the Oratory of the Oblate Fathers in Inchicore on 16 February 1993. In the previous year our daughter Bernadette started working with British

Midlands, followed this year by our son Archie. They both took up posts in Derby, Heathrow and Dublin. If they were working in Dublin they were able to come home very frequently which Bernie and I liked with the added bonus of the staff concessions. Perhaps their involvement in Air Scouting activities prompted them to work for an airline.

Within Scouting, the highlight of this year was 'Ballyfin '93'. Hosted by CBSI in co-operation with FISA, this Jamboree took place between 27 July and 5 August. It was officially opened by President Mary Robinson and attended by 7,000 Scouts and Venturers from Ireland and abroad. For the very first time, Cub Scouts who were doing their link badge were eligible to take part. This gave them an opportunity to see the Scout programme in action and hopefully encourage them to continue in Scouting. Kiernan Gildea was Camp Chief and in his opening address he gave credit to all the people, from many units, who had planned and laboured over the previous three years to bring the camp alive and make it a reality.

The 35th Dublin was not found wanting in providing much-needed help in the construction and manning of sub-camps. Our son Martin and his wife Hillary were deeply involved in the design and building of a full-size monastery enclosure and I had a small involvement by way of preparing drawings and a model. Bernie and I visited the site mid-camp and we were very impressed with everything we saw. Little did we know that six years later we would re-locate permanently to Mountrath, only ten minutes drive from Ballyfin and that we would regularly visit there for enjoyable walks around the lake.

Family and professional commitments, and other considerations, prompted me to resign my post as National Commissioner for Air Activities. With a very strong team of leaders enthusiastically supporting and implementing the Air Activities Progress Scheme, I felt it was the right time to step aside and allow the very vibrant NAAT to further develop Air Activities for all sections nationally. In presenting my resignation to the National Executive Board, I proposed Mary Fricker as my successor and the Board, at their September meeting ratified this. Mary was an experienced leader with the 35th, Assistant Regional Commissioner and a member of the National Training Team and had become actively involved in the Air Activities Programme. I was confident she and her successors would develop the programme with the support of the team.

The structure within the Scouting organisation nationally has changed many times since the idea of introducing Air Activities came into being in the early 1980s and it is very rewarding to see that this continues to be a part of the overall programme within the movement to this day. It is also very satisfying to know that introducing aeronautical subjects had a lasting effect on some young people who today are professional airmen with careers as engineers or pilots. My son Archie currently is a pilot with British Airways flying the Boeing 747, better known as the 'Jumbo'.

The 35th Dublin, St Theresa's Unit has been in existence, uninterrupted for eighty years and long may it continue. It is now one hundred years since Major General Robert

Baden-Powell of Gilwell tried out his ideas at Brownsea Island with twenty boys. As everybody knows, the movement has spread throughout the world and has been to the forefront in helping in the development of young people and towards the creation of a fair, just and equal society for everyone.

On a personal note, it is gratifying to be witness to a fourth generation of Raeside's, that is my grandchildren Eoin and Aoife and their parents Martin and Hillary being actively involved in Scouting in Ireland with the same unit I joined all those years ago. My grand-daughter Sophia was also involved in Scotland where it all began within my family with her great-grandfather. My daughter Berni is currently Akela, or Cub Scout Leader with the Castle Donington Cubs, Windmill Park, which is part of Loughborough District Scouts and her son Conor is a member of the Cub Pack. Scouting has been a big part of my life and beneficial in many ways in my formative years and adult life. Perhaps I was fortunate to have been involved with an exceptionally well-organised unit. As I reflect on my experiences, I have great admiration for all the dedicated and committed people, past and present who tirelessly promote and actively pursue the objectives of the organisation.